Cite Right

Chicago Guides
to *Writing*, Editing,
and Publishing

Cite Right

A Quick Guide to Citation Styles—
MLA, APA, Chicago, the Sciences,
Professions, and More

Charles Lipson

The University of Chicago Press CHICAGO AND LONDON

The University of Chicago Press, Chicago 60637
The University of Chicago Press, Ltd., London
© 2006 by Charles Lipson

15 14 13 12 11 10 09 08 07   4 5

ISBN-13: 978-0-226-48474-7 (cloth)
ISBN-13: 978-0-226-48475-4 (paper)
ISBN-10: 0-226-48474-2 (cloth)
ISBN-10: 0-226-48475-0 (paper)

Library of Congress Cataloging-in-Publication Data

Lipson, Charles.
    Cite right : a quick guide to citation styles—MLA,
APA, Chicago, the sciences, professions, and more /
Charles Lipson.
        p. cm.—(Chicago guides to writing, editing,
    and publishing)
    Includes index.
    ISBN-13: 978-0-226-48474-7 (cloth : alk. paper)
    ISBN-10: 0-226-48474-2 (cloth : alk. paper)
    ISBN-13: 978-0-226-48475-4 (pbk. : alk. paper)
    ISBN-10: 0-226-48475-0 (pbk. : alk. paper)
    1. Bibliographical citations. I. Title. II. Series.
    PN171.F56L55 2006
    808′.027—dc22   2005035580

⊗ The paper used in this publication meets the
minimum requirements of the American National
Standard for Information Sciences—Permanence of
Paper for Printed Library Materials, ANSI z39.48-
1992.

To the reference

librarians who have

helped countless readers,

including me

CONTENTS

Citations: An Overview

1 WHY CITE?

There are three reasons to cite the materials you use:

- To give credit to others' work and ideas, whether you agree with them or not. When you use their words, you must give them credit by using both quotation marks and citations.
- To show readers the materials on which you base your analysis, your narrative, or your conclusions.
- To guide readers to the materials you have used so they can examine it for themselves. Their interest might be to confirm your work, to challenge it, or simply to explore it further.

Taken together, these citations fully disclose your sources. That's important for academic integrity in several ways.

First, good citations parcel out credit. Some belongs to you for the original work you did; you need to take full responsibility for it. Some belongs to others for their words, ideas, data, drawings, or other work. You need to acknowledge it, openly and explicitly.

Second, if you relied on others' work in order to tell your story, explain your topic, or document your conclusions, you need to say exactly what you used. Take a simple paper about World War I. No one writing today learned about it firsthand. What we know, we learned by reading books and articles, by examining original documents and news reports, by listening to oral histories, by reviewing data compiled by military historians, and perhaps by viewing photographs or movies. When we write about the war, then, we should say how we acquired our information. The only exception is "commonly known information," something that everyone in the field clearly understands and that does not require any substantiation.[1] There's no need for a footnote to prove Woodrow Wilson was actually president of the United States. But if you referred to his speech declaring war, you would need a proper citation. If you used his words, you'd need quotation marks, too.

---

1. What counts as common knowledge depends on your audience.

Third, your readers may want to pursue a particular issue you cover. Citations should lead them to the right sources, whether those are books, interviews, archival documents, Web sites, poems, or paintings. That guidance serves several purposes. Skeptical readers may doubt the basis for your work or your conclusions. Others may simply want to double-check them or do more research on the topic. Your citations should point the way.

What citations should *not* do is prance about, showing off your knowledge without adding to the reader's. That's just bragging.

Beyond this question of style (and good manners), there is the basic issue of honesty. *Citations should never mislead your readers.* There are lots of ways to mislead or misdirect your readers; accurate citations avoid them. For example, they should not imply you read books or articles when you really didn't. They should not imply you spent days in the archives deciphering original documents when you actually read them in an edited book or, worse, when you "borrowed" the citation from a scholar who *did* study the originals. Of course, it's fine to cite that author or an edited collection. That's accurate. It's fine to burrow into the archives and read the original yourself. It's dishonest, though, to write citations that only pretend you did.

Good citations should reveal your sources, not conceal them. They should honestly show the research you conducted. That means they should give credit where credit is due, disclose the materials on which you base your work, and guide readers to that material so they can explore it further. Citations like these accurately reflect your work and that of others. They show the ground on which you stand.

2 THE BASICS OF CITATION

Acknowledging your sources is crucial to doing honest academic work. That means citing them properly, using one of several styles. The one you choose depends on your field, your professor's advice if you are a student, and your own preferences.

There are three major citation styles:

- Chicago (or Turabian), used in many fields
- MLA, used in the humanities
- APA, used in social sciences, education, engineering, and business

Several sciences have also developed their own distinctive styles:

- CSE for the biological sciences
- AMA for the biomedical sciences, medicine, and nursing
- ACS for chemistry
- AIP for physics, plus other styles for astrophysics and astronomy
- AMS for mathematics and computer sciences

Legal citations are different from any of these. So are anthropology citations.

I will cover each one, providing clear directions and plenty of examples so you won't have any trouble writing correct citations. That way, you can concentrate on your paper, not on the type of citation you're using. I'll cover each style separately so you can turn directly to the one you need. Using this information, you'll be able to cite books, articles, Web sites, films, musical performances, government documents—whatever you use in your papers.

Why would you ever want to use different citation styles? Why can't you just pick one and stick with it? Because different fields won't let you. They have designed citation styles to meet their special needs, whether it's genetics or German, and you'll just have to use them. In some sciences, for instance, proper citations list only the author, journal, and pages. They omit the article's title. If you did that in the humanities or social sciences, you'd be incorrect because proper citations for those fields *require* the title. Go figure.

Compare these bibliographic citations for an article of mine:

Chicago   Lipson, Charles. "Why Are Some International Agreements Informal?" *International Organization* 45 (Autumn 1991): 495–538.

APA   Lipson, C. (1991). Why are some international agreements informal? *International Organization, 45*, 495–538.

ACS   Lipson, C. *Int. Org.* **1991**, 45, 495.

None of these is complicated, but they *are* different. When you leave the chemistry lab to take a course on Shakespeare, you'll leave behind your citation style as well as your beakers. Not to worry. For chemistry papers, just turn to chapter 9. For Shakespeare, turn to chapter 4, which covers MLA citations for the humanities. Both chapters include lots of examples, presented in simple tables, so it won't be "double, double toil and trouble."

Despite their differences, *all these citation styles have the same basic goals*:

• to identify and credit the sources you use; and
• to give readers specific information so they can go to these sources themselves, if they wish.

Fortunately, the different styles include a lot of the same information. That means you can write down the same things as you take notes, without worrying about what kind of citations you will ultimately use. You should write down that information as soon as you start taking notes on a new book or article. If you photocopy an article, write all the reference information on the first page. If you do it first, you won't forget. You'll need it later for citations.

How these citations will ultimately look depends on which style you use. Chicago notes are either complete citations or shortened versions plus a complete description in the bibliography or in a previous note. Their name comes from their original source, *The Chicago Manual of Style*, published by the University of Chicago Press. This format is sometimes called "Turabian" after a popular book based on that style, Kate Turabian's *A Manual for Writers of Term Papers, Theses, and Dissertations.*[1]

---

1. Kate Turabian, *A Manual for Writers of Term Papers, Theses, and Dissertations*, 6th ed. (Chicago: University of Chicago Press, 1996); *The Chicago Manual of Style*, 15th ed. (Chicago: University of Chicago Press, 2003).

If you use complete-citation notes, you might not need a bibliography at all since the first note for each item includes all the necessary data. If you use the shortened form, though, you definitely need a bibliography since the notes skip vital information.

Whether you use complete-citation notes or the shortened version, you can place them either at the bottom of each page or at the end of the document. Footnotes and endnotes are identical, except for their placement. Footnotes appear on the same page as the citation in the text. Endnotes are bunched together at the end of the paper, article, chapter, or book. Word processors give you an easy choice between the two.

MLA, APA, and the science citation styles were developed to provide alternative ways of referencing materials. They use in-text citations such as (Stewart 154) or (Stewart, 2004) with full information provided only in a reference list at the end.[2] Because these in-text citations are brief, they require a full bibliography. I'll describe each style in detail and provide lots of examples, just as I will for Chicago citations.

In case you are wondering about the initials: APA stands for the American Psychological Association, which uses this style in its professional journals. MLA stands for the Modern Language Association. Both styles have been adopted well beyond their original fields. APA is widely used in the social sciences, MLA in the humanities. Chicago citations are widely used in both. I will discuss the science styles (and what their initials mean) a little later.

Your department, school, or publisher may prefer one style or even require it, or they might leave it up to you. Check on that as soon as you begin handing in papers with citations. Why not do it consistently from the beginning?

Tip on selecting a citation style: Check with your teachers in each class to find out what style citations they prefer. Then use that style consistently.

Speaking of consistency . . . it's an important aspect of footnoting. Stick with the same abbreviations, capitalizations, and don't mix styles within a paper. It's easy to write "Volume" in one footnote, "Vol." in another, and "vol." in a third. We all do it, and then we have to correct it. We all

---

2. Reference lists are similar to bibliographies, but there are some technical differences. In later chapters, I'll explain the details (and nomenclature) for each style. To avoid a needless proliferation of citation styles, I include only the most common ones in each academic field.

abbreviate "chapter" as both "chap." and "ch." Just try your best the first time around and then go back and fix the mistakes when you revise. That's why they invented the search-and-replace function.

My goal here is to provide a one-stop reference so that you can handle nearly all citation issues you'll face, regardless of which style you use and what kinds of items you cite. For each style, I'll show you how to cite books, articles, unpublished papers, Web sites, and lots more. For specialized documents, such as musical scores or scientific preprints, I show citations only in the fields that actually use them. Physicists often cite preprints, but they don't cite Beethoven. The physics chapter reflects those needs. Students in the humanities not only cite Beethoven; they cite dance performances, plays, and poems. I have included MLA citations for all of them. In case you need to cite something well off the beaten path, I'll explain where to find additional information for each style.

HANGING INDENTS

One final point about shared bibliographic style. Most bibliographies— Chicago, MLA, APA, and some of the sciences—use a special style known as "hanging indents." This applies only to the bibliography and not to footnotes or endnotes. It is the opposite of regular paragraph indention, where the first line is indented and the rest are regular length. In a hanging indent, the first line of each citation is regular length and the rest are indented. For example:

> Rothenberg, Gunther E. "Maurice of Nassau, Gustavus Adolphus, Raimondo Montecuccoli, and the 'Military Revolution' of the Seventeenth Century." In *Makers of Modern Strategy from Machiavelli to the Nuclear Age*, edited by Peter Paret, 32–63. Princeton, NJ: Princeton University Press, 1986.
> Spooner, Frank C. *Risks at Sea: Amsterdam Insurance and Maritime Europe, 1766–1780*. Cambridge: Cambridge University Press, 1983.

There's a good reason for this unusual format. Hanging indents are designed to make it easy to skim down the list of references and see the authors' names. To remind you to use this format, I'll use it myself when I illustrate references in the citation styles that use it. (The only ones that don't use hanging indents are science styles with numbered citations and legal citations. It's actually not complicated, and I'll explain it later.)

To make the authors' names stand out further, most bibliographies list their last names first. If an author's name is repeated, however, the styles differ. APA repeats the full name for each citation. MLA uses three hyphens, followed by a period. Chicago uses three em dashes (that is, long dashes), followed by a period.[3]

> Lipson, Charles. *Barbecue, Cole Slaw, and Extra Hot Sauce.* Midnight, MS: Hushpuppy, 2006.
> ———. *More Gumbo, Please.* Thibodeaux, LA: Andouille Press, 2005.

You can arrange hanging indents easily on your word processor. Go to the format feature and, within it, the section on paragraphs. Choose hanging indentation instead of regular or none.

WHERE TO FIND MORE

So far, we have covered some basic issues that apply to most citation styles. There are, of course, lots more questions, some that apply to all styles and some that apply only to one or two. Rather than cover these questions now, I'll handle them in the chapters on individual citation styles and in a final chapter on Frequently Asked Questions (FAQs).

If you have questions that aren't covered in the chapter on your citation style, be sure to check the FAQ chapter. If you still have questions, you can always go to the reference books for each style. Most styles have them (but not all). I'll list them in the chapters for individual styles.

ON TO THE NUTS AND BOLTS

I have organized the references so they are most convenient for you, putting all the documentation for each style in its own chapter.

Chapter 3: Chicago (or Turabian) citations
Chapter 4: MLA citations for the humanities
Chapter 5: APA citations for the social sciences, education, engineering, and business

---

3. Because em dashes are longer than hyphens, they show up differently on-screen and in print. The em dashes show up as a solid line, the hyphens as separate dashes. Three em dashes: ———. Three hyphens: ---. Frankly, you don't need to worry about this for your papers. Use the preferred one if you can, but either is fine.

Chapter 6: AAA citations for anthropology and ethnography
Chapter 7: CSE citations for the biological sciences
Chapter 8: AMA citations for the biomedical sciences, medicine, and
    nursing
Chapter 9: ACS citations for chemistry
Chapter 10: Physics, astrophysics, and astronomy citations
Chapter 11: Mathematics and computer science citations
Chapter 12: *Bluebook* legal citations
Chapter 13: ALWD legal citations

Fortunately, they're very straightforward. They're mostly examples, showing you how to cite specific kinds of sources, such as the third edition of a popular book or a chapter in an edited volume. I've included lots of examples of electronic documents, too, from Weblogs and databases to electronic versions of print documents.

Don't bother trying to memorize any of these styles. There are simply too many minor details. Just follow the tables, and you'll be able to handle different sources—from journal articles to Web pages—in whichever style you need to use. Later, as you write more papers, you'll become familiar with the style you use most.

After explaining each style, I'll answer some common questions that apply to all of them. That's in chapter 14. Now, let's see how to do citations and bibliographies in the specific style you want to use.

Citations in Every Format:
A Quick Guide

3 CHICAGO (OR TURABIAN) CITATIONS

Chicago citations are based on the authoritative *Chicago Manual of Style*. The manual, now in its fifteenth edition, is the bible for references and academic style. A briefer version, covering most aspects of student papers, is Kate Turabian's *A Manual for Writers of Term Papers, Theses, and Dissertations*. This section, however, should cover all you need to document your sources, even if they're unusual.

FULL NOTES, SHORT NOTES, AND BIBLIOGRAPHY

Chicago-style notes come in two flavors, and I include both in this section.[1]

1. A complete first note + short follow-up notes.
   The first note for any item is a full one, giving complete information about the book, article, or other document. Subsequent entries for that item are brief. There is no need for a bibliography since all the information is covered in the first note.
2. Short notes only + bibliography.
   All notes are brief. Full information about the sources appears only in the bibliography.

This means there are three ways to cite individual items. All of them are illustrated in this appendix.

A. Full first notes
B. Short notes
C. Bibliographic entries

---

1. *The Chicago Manual of Style* and Turabian also describe another style, the author-date system. These citations appear in parentheses in the text, listing the author and the date of publication. For example: (Larmore 2006). Full citations appear in a reference list at the end. For simplicity, I have omitted this style since it is similar to APA, discussed in chapter 5.

The first flavor combines A + B, the second combines B + C.

This section covers everything from edited books to reference works, from sheet music to online databases, and lots of things in between. To make it easy to find what you need, I've listed them here alphabetically, together with the pages they are on. At the end of this section, I answer some question about using this style.

INDEX OF CHICAGO CITATIONS IN THIS CHAPTER

CHICAGO MANUAL OF STYLE: NOTES AND BIBLIOGRAPHY

| Book, one author | Full first note | [99]Charles Lipson, *Reliable Partners: How Democracies Have Made a Separate Peace* (Princeton, NJ: Princeton University Press, 2003), 22–23. |

> ► This is note number 99 and refers to pages 22–23.
> ► Footnotes and endnotes do not have hanging indents. Only the bibliography does.

Short note
[99]Lipson, *Reliable Partners*, 22–23.
> ► Shorten titles to four words or less, if possible.

Bibliography
Lipson, Charles. *Reliable Partners: How Democracies Have Made a Separate Peace.* Princeton, NJ: Princeton University Press, 2003.

Books, several by same author

First note
[99]Gerhard L. Weinberg, *Germany, Hitler, and World War II: Essays in Modern German and World History* (Cambridge: Cambridge University Press, 1995).
[100]Gerhard L. Weinberg, *A World at Arms: A Global History of World War II* (Cambridge: Cambridge University Press, 1994).

Short note
[99]Weinberg, *Germany, Hitler, and World War II.*
[100]Weinberg, *World at Arms.*

Bibliography
Weinberg, Gerhard L. *Germany, Hitler, and World War II: Essays in Modern German and World History.* Cambridge: Cambridge University Press, 1995.
———. *A World at Arms: A Global History of World War II.* Cambridge: Cambridge University Press, 1994.
> ► The repetition of the author's name uses three em dashes (which are simply long dashes), followed by a period. You can find em dashes by digging around in Microsoft Word. Go to "Insert," then "Symbols," then "Special Characters." After you do it once, you can simply copy and paste it. If, for some reason, you can't find the em dash, just use three hyphens.
> ► List works for each author alphabetically, by title. In alphabetizing, skip any initial article: *a, an, the.*

Book, multiple authors	First note	[99] Dan Reiter and Allan C. Stam, *Democracies at War* (Princeton, NJ: Princeton University Press, 2002), 15–26.
	Short note	[99] Reiter and Stam, *Democracies at War*, 15–26. ▸ Titles with four words or less are not shortened.
	Bibliography	Reiter, Dan, and Allan C. Stam. *Democracies at War*. Princeton, NJ: Princeton University Press, 2002. ▸ List up to ten coauthors in the bibliography. If there are more, list the first seven, followed by "et al."
Book, multiple editions	First note	[99] William Strunk Jr. and E. B. White, *The Elements of Style*, 4th ed. (New York: Longman, 2000), 12.
	Short note	[99] Strunk and White, *Elements of Style*, 12. ▸ To keep the note short, the title doesn't include the initial article (~~The~~ *Elements of Style*) or the edition number.
	Bibliography	Strunk, William, Jr., and E. B. White. *The Elements of Style*. 4th ed. New York: Longman, 2000.
Book, edited	First note	[99] Francis Robinson, ed., *Cambridge Illustrated History of the Islamic World* (Cambridge: Cambridge University Press, 1996). [99] David Taras, Frits Pannekoek, and Maria Bakardjieva, eds., *How Canadians Communicate* (Calgary, AB: University of Calgary Press, 2003). ▸ Use standard two-letter abbreviations for Canadian provinces.
	Short note	[99] Robinson, *History of Islamic World*. ▸ Choose the most relevant words when shortening the title. Also, drop the abbreviation for editor. [99] Taras, Pannekoek, and Bakardjieva, *How Canadians Communicate*.

	Bibliography	Robinson, Francis, ed. *Cambridge Illustrated History of the Islamic World.* Cambridge· Cambridge University Press, 1996. Taras, David, Frits Pannekoek, and Maria Bakardjieva, eds. *How Canadians Communicate.* Calgary, AB: University of Calgary Press, 2003.
Book, anonymous or no author	First note	[99]Anonymous, *Through Our Enemies' Eyes: Osama Bin Laden, Radical Islam, and the Future of America* (Washington, DC: Brassey's, 2003). [99] *Golden Verses of the Pythagoreans* (Whitefish, MT: Kessinger, 2003).
	Short note	[99]Anonymous, *Through Our Enemies' Eyes.* [99]*Golden Verses of Pythagoreans.*
	Bibliography	Anonymous, *Through Our Enemies' Eyes: Osama Bin Laden, Radical Islam, and the Future of America.* Washington, DC: Brassey's, 2003. *Golden Verses of the Pythagoreans.* Whitefish, MT: Kessinger, 2003. ► If a book lists "anonymous" as the author, then that word should be included. If no author is listed, then you may list "anonymous" or simply begin with the title.
Book, online	First note	[99]Charles Dickens, *Great Expectations* (1860–61; Project Gutenberg, 1998), etext 1400, http://www.gutenberg.net/etext98/grexp10.txt. ► The etext number is helpful but not essential.
	Short note	[99]Dickens, *Great Expectations.*
	Bibliography	Dickens, Charles. *Great Expectations* (1860–61; Project Gutenberg, 1998). Etext 1400. http://www.gutenberg.net/etext98/grexp10.txt.
Multivolume work	First note	[99]Otto Pflanze, *Bismarck and the Development of Germany,* 3 vols. (Princeton, NJ: Princeton University Press, 1963–90), 1:153.
	Short note	[99]Pflanze, *Bismarck,* 1:153.

Multivolume work (*continued*)	Bibliography	Pflanze, Otto. *Bismarck and the Development of Germany.* 3 vols. Princeton, NJ: Princeton University Press, 1963–90.
Single volume in a multivolume work	First note	[99]Otto Pflanze, *Bismarck and the Development of Germany*, vol. 3, *The Period of Fortification, 1880–1898* (Princeton, NJ: Princeton University Press, 1990), 237. [99]Akira Iriye, *The Globalizing of America*, Cambridge History of American Foreign Relations, edited by Warren I. Cohen, vol. 3 (Cambridge: Cambridge University Press, 1993), 124. ▸ Pflanze wrote all three volumes. Iriye wrote only the third volume in a series edited by Cohen.
	Short note	[99]Pflanze, *Bismarck*, 3:237. [99]Iriye, *Globalizing of America*, 124.
	Bibliography	Pflanze, Otto. *Bismarck and the Development of Germany.* Vol. 3, *The Period of Fortification, 1880–1898.* Princeton, NJ: Princeton University Press, 1990. Iriye, Akira. *The Globalizing of America.* Cambridge History of American Foreign Relations, edited by Warren I. Cohen, vol. 3. Cambridge: Cambridge University Press, 1993.
Reprint of earlier edition	First note	[99]Jacques Barzun, *Simple and Direct: A Rhetoric for Writers*, rev. ed. (1985; repr., Chicago: University of Chicago Press, 1994), 27. [99]Adam Smith, *An Inquiry into the Nature and Causes of the Wealth of Nations* (1776), ed. Edwin Cannan (Chicago: University of Chicago Press, 1976). ▸ The year 1776 appears immediately after the title because that's when Smith's original work appeared. The editor, Edwin Cannan, worked only on its modern publication. The Barzun volume, by contrast, is simply a reprint so the original year appears as part of the publication information.

Short note   ⁹⁹Barzun, *Simple and Direct*, 27.
⁹⁹Smith, *Wealth of Nations*, vol. I, bk. IV, chap. II: 477.

> This modern edition of Smith is actually a single volume, but it retains the volume numbering of the 1776 original. You could simply cite the page number, but the full citation helps readers with other editions.

Bibliography   Barzun, Jacques. *Simple and Direct: A Rhetoric for Writers*. 1985. Reprint, Chicago: University of Chicago Press, 1994.
Smith, Adam. *An Inquiry into the Nature and Causes of the Wealth of Nations*. 1776. Edited by Edwin Cannan. Chicago: University of Chicago Press, 1976.

Translated volume

First note   ⁹⁹Max Weber, *The Protestant Ethic and the Spirit of Capitalism* (1904–5), trans. Talcott Parsons (New York: Charles Scribner's Sons, 1958), 176–77.
⁹⁹Alexis de Tocqueville, *Democracy in America* (1835), ed. J. P. Mayer, trans. George Lawrence (New York: HarperCollins, 2000).

> Translator and editor are listed in the order they appear on the book's title page.

⁹⁹Seamus Heaney, trans., *Beowulf: A New Verse Translation* (New York: Farrar, Straus and Giroux, 2000).

> For *Beowulf*, the translator's name appears before the book title because Heaney's is the only name on the title page. (The poem is anonymous.) The same treatment would be given to an editor or compiler whose name appeared alone on the title page.

Short note   ⁹⁹Weber, *Protestant Ethic*, 176–77.
⁹⁹Tocqueville, *Democracy in America*.
⁹⁹*Beowulf.*

> Or

⁹⁹Heaney, *Beowulf.*

Translated volume (*continued*)	Bibliography	Weber, Max. *The Protestant Ethic and the Spirit of Capitalism.* 1904–5. Translated by Talcott Parsons. New York: Charles Scribner's Sons, 1958.
		Tocqueville, Alexis de. *Democracy in America.* 1835. Edited by J. P. Mayer. Translated by George Lawrence. New York: HarperCollins, 2000.
		Heaney, Seamus, trans. *Beowulf: A New Verse Translation.* New York: Farrar, Straus and Giroux, 2000.
Chapter in edited book	First note	[99]Robert Keohane, "The Demand for International Regimes," in *International Regimes*, ed. Stephen Krasner, 55–67 (Ithaca, NY: Cornell University Press, 1983).
	Short note	[99]Keohane, "Demand for International Regimes," 56–67.
	Bibliography	Keohane, Robert. "The Demand for International Regimes." In *International Regimes*, edited by Stephen Krasner, 56–67. Ithaca, NY: Cornell University Press, 1983.
Journal article, one author	First note	[99]Charles Lipson, "Why Are Some International Agreements Informal?" *International Organization* 45 (Autumn 1991): 495–538.
	Short note	[99]Lipson, "International Agreements," 495–538.
	Bibliography	Lipson, Charles. "Why Are Some International Agreements Informal?" *International Organization* 45 (Autumn 1991): 495–538.
Journal article, multiple authors	First note	[99]William G. Thomas III and Edward L. Ayers, "An Overview: The Differences Slavery Made; A Close Analysis of Two American Communities," *American Historical Review* 108 (December 2003): 1299–307.
	Short note	[99]Thomas and Ayers, "Differences Slavery Made," 1299–307.

	Bibliography	Thomas, William G., III, and Edward L. Ayers. "An Overview: The Differences Slavery Made; A Close Analysis of Two American Communities." *American Historical Review* 108 (December 2003): 1299–307.
Journal article, online	First note	[99]Christopher Small, "Why Doesn't the Whole World Love Chamber Music?" *American Music* 19:3 (Autumn 2001): 340–59. http://links.jstor.org/sici?sici=0734-4392%28200123%2919%3A3%3C340%3AWDTWWL%3E2.0.CO%3B2-J (accessed March 15, 2004).
	Short note	[99]Small, "Chamber Music," 340–59.
	Bibliography	Small, Christopher. "Why Doesn't the Whole World Love Chamber Music?" *American Music* 19:3 (Autumn 2001): 340–59. http://links.jstor.org/sici?sici=0734-4392%28200123%2919%3A3%3C340%3AWDTWWL%3E2.0.CO%3B2-J (accessed March 15, 2004).
Journal article, foreign language	First note	[99]Zvi Uri Ma'oz, "Y a-t-il des juifs sans synagogue?" *Revue des Études Juives* 163 (juillet–décembre 2004): 483–93.
		▶ Or
		[99]Zvi Uri Ma'oz, "Y a-t-il des juifs sans synagogue?" [Are there Jews without a synagogue?] *Revue des Études Juives* 163 (juillet–décembre 2004): 483–93.
	Short note	[99]Ma'oz, "Y a-t-il des juifs sans synagogue?" 483–93.
	Bibliography	Ma'oz, Zvi Uri. "Y a-t-il des juifs sans synagogue?" *Revue des Études Juives* 163 (juillet–décembre 2004): 483–93.
		▶ Or
		Ma'oz, Zvi Uri. "Y a-t-il des juifs sans synagogue?" [Are there Jews without a synagogue?] *Revue des Études Juives* 163 (juillet–décembre 2004): 483–93.

Newspaper or magazine article, no author	First note	[99] "Report of 9/11 Panel Cites Lapses by C.I.A. and F.B.I.," *New York Times*, July 23, 2003 (national edition), 1. ▸ This refers to page 1. ▸ If the article has a byline and you wish to include the reporter's name, you certainly can: David Johnston, "Report of 9/11 Panel . . ." ▸ Short articles in newsweeklies like *Time* are treated the same as newspaper articles. Longer articles with bylines are treated like journal articles.
	Short note	[99] "Report of 9/11 Panel," *New York Times*, 1. ▸ Since newspapers are usually omitted from the bibliography, use a full citation for the first reference. ▸ Newspapers articles are left out of bibliographies, but you can include an especially important article:
	Bibliography	"Report of 9/11 Panel Cites Lapses by C.I.A. and F.B.I." *New York Times*, July 23, 2003, national edition, 1.
Newspaper or magazine article, with author	First note	[99] Jason Horowitz, "Vatican Official Is Killed by Gunmen in Burundi," *New York Times*, December 30, 2003 (national edition), A9.
	Short note	[99] Horowitz, "Vatican Official Is Killed," A9.
	Bibliography	▸ Newspaper and magazine articles are rarely included in bibliographies.
Newspaper or magazine article, online	First note	[99] Karl Vick, "Iranians Flee Quake-Devastated City," *Washington Post*, December 31, 2003, A01, http://www.washingtonpost.com/wp-dyn/articles/A42890-2003Dec30.html (accessed March 14, 2004).
	Short note	[99] Vick, "Iranians Flee Quake-Devastated City."
	Bibliography	▸ Rarely included.

Review	First note	[99]H. Allen Orr, "What's Not in Your Genes," review of *Nature via Nurture: Genes, Experience, and What Makes Us Human,* by Matt Ridley, *New York Review of Books* 50 (August 14, 2003): 38–40. [99]Zdravko Planinc, review of *Eros and Polis: Desire and Community in Greek Political Theory,* by Paul W. Ludwig, *Perspectives on Politics* 1 (December 2003): 764–65.
	Short note	[99]Orr, "What's Not in Your Genes." [99]Planinc, review of *Eros and Polis.*
	Bibliography	Orr, H. Allen. "What's Not in Your Genes." Review of *Nature via Nurture: Genes, Experience, and What Makes Us Human,* by Matt Ridley. *New York Review of Books* 50 (August 14, 2003): 38–40. Planinc, Zdravko. Review of *Eros and Polis: Desire and Community in Greek Political Theory,* by Paul W. Ludwig. *Perspectives on Politics* 1 (December 2003): 764–65.
Unpublished paper, thesis, or dissertation	First note	[99]Janice Bially-Mattern, "Ordering International Politics: Identity, Crisis, and Representational Force" (paper presented at the Program on International Politics, Economics, and Security, University of Chicago, February 5, 2004), 1–25. [99]Nicole Childs, "The Impact of Hurricane Floyd on the Children of Eastern North Carolina" (master's thesis, Eastern Carolina University, 2002), 24. [99]Soon-Yong Choi, "Optimal Quality Choices: Product Selection in Cable Television Services" (PhD diss., University of Texas, Austin, 1996).
	Short note	[99]Bially-Mattern, "Ordering International Politics." [99]Childs, "Impact of Hurricane Floyd." [99]Choi, "Optimal Quality Choices."
	Bibliography	Bially-Mattern, Janice. "Ordering International Politics: Identity, Crisis, and Representational Force." Paper presented at the Program on International Politics,

Unpublished paper, thesis, or dissertation (*continued*)		Economics, and Security, University of Chicago, February 5, 2004. Childs, Nicole. "The Impact of Hurricane Floyd on the Children of Eastern North Carolina." Master's thesis, Eastern Carolina University, 2002. Choi, Soon-Yong. "Optimal Quality Choices: Product Selection in Cable Television Services." PhD diss., University of Texas, Austin, 1996.
Preprint	First note	[99]Richard Taylor, "On the Meromorphic Continuation of Degree Two L-Functions," preprint, http://abel.math.harvard.edu/~rtaylor/ (accessed January 5, 2004).
	Short note	[99]Taylor, "Meromorphic Continuation."
	Bibliography	Taylor, Richard. "On the Meromorphic Continuation of Degree Two L-Functions," preprint. http://abel.math.harvard.edu/~rtaylor/ (accessed January 5, 2004).
Abstract	First note	[99]Michael Kremer and Alix Peterson Zwane, "Encouraging Private Sector Research for Tropical Agriculture," abstract, *World Development* 33 (January 2005): 87–105. [99]Cecilia Albin, "Negotiating International Cooperation: Global Public Goods and Fairness," *Review of International Studies* 29 (July 2003): 365–85, abstract in *Peace Research Abstracts Journal* 42, publ. nr. 236625 (February 2005): 6.
	Short note	[99]Kremer and Zwane, "Encouraging Private Sector Research," 87–105. [99]Albin, "Negotiating International Cooperation," 6.
	Bibliography	Kremer, Michael, and Alix Peterson Zwane. "Encouraging Private Sector Research for Tropical Agriculture." Abstract. *World Development* 33 (January 2005): 87–105. Albin, Cecilia. "Negotiating International Cooperation: Global Public Goods and

Fairness." *Review of International Studies* 29
(July 2003): 365–85. Abstract in *Peace
Research Abstracts Journal* 42, publ. nr.
236625 (February 2005): 6.

Microfilm, microfiche	First note	[99]Martin Luther King Jr., *FBI File*, ed. David J. Garrow (Frederick, MD: University Publications of America, 1984), microform, 16 reels. [99]Alice Irving Abbott, *Circumstantial Evidence* (New York: W. B. Smith, 1882), in *American Fiction, 1774–1910* (Woodbridge, CT: Gale/Primary Source Microfilm, 1998), reel A-1.
	Short note	[99]King, *FBI File*, 11:23–24. [99]Abbott, *Circumstantial Evidence*, 73.
	Bibliography	King, Martin Luther, Jr., *FBI File*. Edited by David J. Garrow. Frederick, MD: University Publications of America, 1984. Microform. 16 reels. Abbott, Alice Irving. *Circumstantial Evidence*. New York: W. B. Smith, 1882. In *American Fiction, 1774–1910*. Reel A-1. Woodbridge, CT: Gale/Primary Source Microfilm, 1998. ▶ You can omit any mention of microfilm or microfiche if it simply preserves a source in its original form. Just cite the work as if it were the published version. So, to cite the Abbott book: Abbott, Alice Irving. *Circumstantial Evidence*. New York: W. B. Smith, 1882.
Archival materials and manuscript collections, hard copies and online	First note	[99]Isaac Franklin to R. C. Ballard, February 28, 1831. Series 1.1, folder 1, Rice Ballard Papers, Southern Historical Collection, Wilson Library, University of North Carolina, Chapel Hill. ▶ Here is the order of items within the citation: 1. Author and brief description of the item 2. Date, if possible 3. Identification number for item or manuscript 4. Title of the series or collection 5. Library (or depository) and its location; for well-known libraries and archives, the location may be omitted.

Archival
materials
(*continued*)

[99]Mary Swift Lamson, "An Account of the Beginning of the B.Y.W.C.A.," MS, [n.d.], and accompanying letter, 1891. Series I, I-A-2, Boston YWCA Papers, Schlesinger Library, Radcliffe Institute for Advanced Study, Harvard University.

▶ "MS" = manuscript = papers (plural: "MSS")

[99]Sigismundo Taraval, Journal recounting Indian uprisings in Baja California [handwritten ms.], ¶ 23, 1734–1737. Edward E. Ayer Manuscript Collection No. 1240, Newberry Library, Chicago, IL.

▶ This journal has numbered paragraphs. Page numbers, paragraphs, or other identifiers aid readers.

[99]Horatio Nelson Taft, Diary, February 20, 1862, p. 149 (vol. 1, January 1, 1861–April 11, 1862). Manuscript Division, Library of Congress, http://memory.loc.gov/ammem/tafthtml/tafthome.html (accessed May 30, 2004).

[99]Henrietta Szold to Rose Jacobs, February 3, 1932. Reel 1, book 1, Rose Jacobs–Alice L. Seligsberg Collection, Judaica Microforms, Brandeis Library, Waltham, MA.

▶ Abbreviations: When a collection's name and location are often repeated, they may be abbreviated after the first use:

[99]Henrietta Szold to Rose Jacobs, March 9, 1936. A/125/112, Central Zionist Archives, Jerusalem (hereafter cited as CZA).

[100]Szold to Eva Stern, July 27, 1936. A/125/912, CZA.

Short note

[99]Isaac Franklin to R. C. Ballard, February 28, 1831. Series 1.1, folder 1, Rice Ballard Papers.

▶ Short-form citation varies for archival items. The main concerns are readers' convenience and the proximity of full information in nearby notes.

[99]Mary Swift Lamson, "Beginning of the B.Y.W.C.A.," MS, [1891]. Boston YWCA Papers, Schlesinger Library.

[99] Sigismundo Taraval, Journal recounting Indian uprisings in Baja California. Edward E. Ayer Manuscript Collection, Newberry Library.

▶ Or

[99] Taraval, Journal. Ayer MS Collection, Newberry Library.

[99] Horatio Nelson Taft, Diary, February 20, 1862, 149.

[99] Henrietta Szold to Rose Jacobs, February 3, 1932. Reel 1, book 1, Rose Jacobs–Alice L. Seligsberg Collection.

[100] Szold to Jacobs, March 9, 1936. A/125/112, CZA.

[101] Szold to Eva Stern, July 27, 1936. A/125/912, CZA.

Bibliography   Rice Ballard Papers. Southern Historical Collection. Wilson Library. University of North Carolina, Chapel Hill.

▶ In footnotes and endnotes, the specific archival item is usually listed first because it is the most important element in the note. For example: Isaac Franklin to R. C. Ballard, February 28, 1831. In bibliographies, however, the collection itself is usually listed first because it is more important. Individual items are not mentioned in the bibliography *unless* only one item is cited from a particular collection.

Boston YWCA Papers. Schlesinger Library. Radcliffe Institute for Advanced Study, Harvard University.

▶ Or

Lamson, Mary Swift. "An Account of the Beginning of the B.Y.W.C.A." MS, [n.d.], and accompanying letter. 1891. Boston YWCA Papers. Schlesinger Library. Radcliffe Institute for Advanced Study, Harvard University.

▶ If Lamson's account is the only item cited from these papers, then it would be listed in the bibliography.

Archival
materials
(*continued*)
		Ayer, Edward E., Manuscript Collection.
		    Newberry Library. Chicago, IL.
		Taft, Horatio Nelson. Diary. Vol. 1, January 1,
		    1861–April 11, 1862. Manuscript Division,
		    Library of Congress, http://memory.loc.gov/
		    ammem/tafthtml/tafthome.html (accessed
		    May 30, 2004).
		Rose Jacobs–Alice L. Seligsberg Collection.
		    Judaica Microforms. Brandeis Library.
		    Waltham, MA.
		Central Zionist Archives, Jerusalem.

Encyclopedia,
hard copy
and online
	First note	[99] *Encyclopaedia Britannica*, 15th ed., s.vv.
		"Balkans: History," "World War I."
		▶ s.v. (*sub verbo*) means "under the word." Plural:
		    s.vv.
		▶ You must include the edition but, according to
		    the *Chicago Manual of Style*, you can omit the
		    publisher, location, and page numbers for
		    well-known references like *Encyclopaedia
		    Britannica*.
		
		[99] *Encyclopaedia Britannica Online*, s.v.
		"Balkans," http://search.eb.com/eb/article
		?eu=119645 (accessed January 2, 2004).
		[99] George Graham, "Behaviorism," in *Stanford
		Encyclopedia of Philosophy*, http://plato
		.stanford.edu/entries/behaviorism/ (accessed
		January 3, 2004).
		▶ Or
		[99] *Stanford Encyclopedia of Philosophy*,
		"Behaviorism" (by George Graham), in http://
		plato.stanford.edu/entries/behaviorism/
		(accessed January 3, 2004).

	Short note	[99] *Encyclopaedia Britannica*, s.v. "World War I." [99] Graham, "Behaviorism." ▶ Or [99] *Stanford Encyclopedia*, "Behaviorism."
	Bibliography	*Encyclopaedia Britannica*. 15th ed. s.vv. "Balkans: History." "World War I."

Encyclopaedia Britannica Online. s.v. "Balkans."
   http://search.eb.com/eb/article?eu=119645
   (accessed January 2, 2004).
Graham, George. "Behaviorism." In *Stanford
   Encyclopedia of Philosophy.* http://plato
   .stanford.edu/entries/behaviorism/
   (accessed January 3, 2004).

▸ Or

Stanford Encyclopedia of Philosophy.
   "Behaviorism" (by George Graham). http://
   plato.stanford.edu/entries/behaviorism/
   (accessed January 3, 2004).

Reference book, hard copy and online	First note	[99]*Reference Guide to World Literature*, 3rd ed., 2 vols., ed. Sara Pendergast and Tom Pendergast (Detroit: St. James Press/Thomson-Gale, 2003). [99]*Reference Guide to World Literature*, 3rd ed., ed. Sara Pendergast and Tom Pendergast, e-book (Detroit: St. James Press, 2003). [99]Edmund Cusick, "The Snow Queen, story by Hans Christian Andersen," in *Reference Guide to World Literature*, 3rd ed., 2 vols., ed. Sara Pendergast and Tom Pendergast (Detroit: St. James Press/Thomson-Gale, 2003), 2:1511–12. [99]"Great Britain: Queen's Speech Opens Parliament," November 26, 2003, *FirstSearch*, Facts On File database, accession no. 2003302680.
	Short note	[99]*Reference Guide to World Literature.* [99]Cusick, "Snow Queen," 2:1511–12. [99]"Great Britain: Queen's Speech."
	Bibliography	*Reference Guide to World Literature.* 3rd ed. 2 vols. Edited by Sara Pendergast and Tom Pendergast. Detroit: St. James Press/Thomson-Gale, 2003. *Reference Guide to World Literature.* 3rd ed. Edited by Sara Pendergast and Tom Pendergast. E-book. Detroit: St. James Press, 2003.

Reference book (*continued*)		Cusick, Edmund. "The Snow Queen, story by Hans Christian Andersen." In *Reference Guide to World Literature*. 3rd ed. 2 vols. Edited by Sara Pendergast and Tom Pendergast, 2:1511–12. Detroit: St. James Press/Thomson-Gale, 2003. "Great Britain: Queen's Speech Opens Parliament." November 26, 2003. *FirstSearch*. Facts On File database. Accession no. 2003302680.
Dictionary, hard copy, online, and CD-ROM	First note	[99]*Merriam-Webster's Collegiate Dictionary*, 11th ed., s.v. "chronology."
		▸ You must include the edition but can omit the publisher, location, and page numbers for well-known references like *Merriam-Webster's*.
		[99]*Compact Edition of the Oxford English Dictionary*, s.vv. "class, *n*.," "state, *n*."
		▸ The words "class" and "state" can be either nouns or verbs, and this reference is to the nouns.
		[99]Dictionary.com, s.v. "status," http:// dictionary.reference.com/search?q=status (accessed February 2, 2004).
		[99]*American Heritage Dictionary of the English Language*, 4th ed., CD-ROM.
	Short note	[99]*Merriam-Webster's*, s.v. "chronology."
		[99]*Compact O.E.D.*, s.vv. "class, *n*.," "state, *n*."
		[99]Dictionary.com, s.v. "status."
		[99]*American Heritage Dictionary of the English Language* on CD-ROM.
		▸ Standard dictionaries are not normally listed in bibliographies, but you may wish to include more specialized reference works:
	Bibliography	*Middle English Dictionary, W.2*, ed. Robert E. Lewis. Ann Arbor: University of Michigan Press, 1999.
		Medieval English Dictionary online. s.v. "boidekin." http://ets.umdl.umich.edu/cgi/ m/mec/med-idx?type=id&id=MED5390.

Bible	First note	⁹⁹Genesis 1:1, 1:3–5, 2:4. ⁹⁹Genesis 1:1, 1:3–5, 2:4 (New Revised Standard Version). ▸ Books of the Bible can be abbreviated: Gen. 1:1. ▸ Abbreviations for the next four books are Exod., Lev., Num., and Deut. Abbreviations for other books are easily found with a Web search for "abbreviations + Bible."
	Short note	⁹⁹Genesis 1:1, 1:3–5, 2:4. ▸ Biblical references are not normally included in the bibliography, but you may wish to include a particular version or translation:
	Bibliography	*Tanakh: The Holy Scriptures: The New JPS Translation according to the Traditional Hebrew Text.* Philadelphia: Jewish Publication Society, 1985. ▸ Thou shalt omit the Divine Author's name.
Speech, academic talk, or course lecture	First note	⁹⁹Henry S. Bienen, "State of the University Speech" (Northwestern University, Evanston, IL, March 6, 2003). ⁹⁹Theda Skocpol, "Voice and Inequality: The Transformation of American Civic Democracy" (Presidential address, American Political Science Association convention, Philadelphia, PA, August 28, 2003). ⁹⁹Gary Sick, lecture on U.S. policy toward Iraq (course on U.S. Foreign Policy Making in the Persian Gulf, Columbia University, New York, March 14, 2004). ▸ The title of Professor Sick's talk is not in quotes because it is a regular course lecture and does not have a specific title. I have given a description, but you could simply call it a lecture and omit the description. For example: Gary Sick, lecture (course on U.S. Foreign . . .).
	Short note	⁹⁹Bienen, "State of the University Speech." ▸ Or, to differentiate it from Bienen's 2002 talk:

Speech or lecture (*continued*)		[99]Bienen, "State of the University Speech," 2003. [99]Skocpol, "Voice and Inequality." [99]Sick, lecture on U.S. policy toward Iraq.
	Bibliography	Bienen, Henry S. "State of the University Speech." Northwestern University, Evanston, IL, March 6, 2003. Skocpol, Theda. "Voice and Inequality: The Transformation of American Civic Democracy." Presidential address, American Political Science Association convention, Philadelphia, PA, August 28, 2003. Sick, Gary. Lecture on U.S. policy toward Iraq. Course on U.S. Foreign Policy Making in the Persian Gulf, Columbia University, New York, March 14, 2004.

Interview, personal, telephone, or in print	First note	[99]V. S. Naipaul, personal interview, May 14, 2005. [99]Tony Blair, telephone interview, February 16, 2005. [99]Anonymous U.S. Marine, recently returned from Iraq, interviewed by author, June 4, 2005. [99]Gloria Macapagal Arroyo, "A Time for Prayer," interview by Michael Schuman, *Time*, July 28, 2003, http://www.time.com/time/nation/article/0,8599,471205,00.html.
	Short note	[99]V. S. Naipaul, personal interview, May 14, 2005. [99]Tony Blair, telephone interview, February 16, 2005. [99]Anonymous U.S. Marine, recently returned from Iraq, interviewed by author, June 4, 2005. [99]Arroyo, "Time for Prayer."

▶ Interviews should be included in the bibliography if they are in print, online, or archived (so that they are available to other researchers). Personal interviews and communications that are *not* accessible to others should be described fully in the notes and omitted from the bibliography. Hence, there is a bibliographic item for Arroyo but none for Naipaul, Blair, or the anonymous U.S. Marine.

	Bibliography	Arroyo, Gloria Macapagal. "A Time for Prayer." Interview by Michael Schuman. *Time*. July 28, 2003. http.//www.time.com/time/nation/ article/0,8599,471205,00.html.

Personal communica-tion	First note	[99]Ron Chernow, personal communication, May 25, 2005. [99]Dr. Adam Rowen, telephone conversation with author, May 29, 2005. [99]Professor Gayle McKeen, letter to author, July 3, 2005. [99]Discussion with senior official at Department of Homeland Security, Washington, DC, June 1, 2005.

> ► Sometimes you may not wish to reveal the source of an interview or conversation, or you may have promised not to reveal your source. If so, then you should (a) reveal as much descriptive data as you can, such as "a police officer who works with an anti-gang unit," instead of just "a police officer" and (b) explain to readers, in some footnote, why you are omitting names, such as "Interviews with State Department officials were conducted with guarantees of anonymity."

	Short note	[99]Ron Chernow, personal communication, May 25, 2005. [99]Dr. Adam Rowen, telephone conversation with author, May 29, 2005. [99]Professor Gayle McKeen, letter to author, July 3, 2005. [99]Discussion with senior official at Department of Homeland Security, Washington, DC, June 1, 2005.

> ► Personal communications are typically omitted from the bibliography, unless they are archived and available to others. For example:

	Bibliography	Kaster, Robert. Comment. October 2004. Posted at http://www.charleslipson.com/Honesty -Reviews.htm.

Poem	First note	[99]Elizabeth Bishop, "The Fish," in *The Complete Poems, 1927–1979* (New York: Noonday Press/Farrar, Straus and Giroux, 1983), 42–44.
	Short note	[99]Bishop, "The Fish," 42–44.
	Bibliography	Bishop, Elizabeth. "The Fish." In *The Complete Poems, 1927–1979*, 42–44. New York: Noonday Press/Farrar, Straus and Giroux, 1983.

Play, text	First note	[99]Shakespeare, *Romeo and Juliet*, 2.1.1–9.
		▸ Refers to act 2, scene 1, lines 1–9.
		▸ If you wish to cite a specific edition, then:
		[99]Shakespeare, *Romeo and Juliet*, ed. Brian Gibbons (London: Methuen, 1980).
	Short note	[99]Shakespeare, *Romeo and Juliet*, 2.1.1–9.
	Bibliography	Shakespeare, *Romeo and Juliet*. Edited by Brian Gibbons. London: Methuen, 1980.

Performance of play or dance	First note	[99]*Kiss*, choreography Susan Marshall, music Arvo Pärt, perf. Cheryl Mann, Tobin Del Cuore, Hubbard Street Dance Chicago, Chicago, March 12, 2004.
		[99]*Topdog/Underdog*, by Suzan Lori-Parks, dir. Amy Morton, perf. K. Todd Freeman, David Rainey, Steppenwolf Theater, Chicago, November 2, 2003.
		▸ If you are concentrating on one person or one position such as director, put that person's name first. For example, if you are concentrating on David Rainey's acting:
		[99]David Rainey, perf., *Topdog/Underdog*, by Suzan Lori-Parks, dir. Amy Morton . . .
	Short note	[99]*Kiss*.
		[99]*Topdog/Underdog*.
	Bibliography	*Kiss*. Choreography Susan Marshall. Music Arvo Pärt. Perf. Cheryl Mann, Tobin Del Cuore. Hubbard Street Dance Chicago, Chicago. March 12, 2004.

Topdog/Underdog. By Suzan Lori-Parks. Dir. Amy Morton. Perf. K. Todd Freeman, David Rainey. Steppenwolf Theater, Chicago. November 2, 2003.

▶ Or, if you are concentrating on Rainey's acting:

Rainey, David, perf. *Topdog/Underdog.* By Suzan Lori-Parks. Dir. Amy Morton . . .

Television program	First note	[99] *Seinfeld*, "The Soup Nazi," episode 116, November 2, 1995.

▶ Or, a fuller citation:

[99] *Seinfeld*, "The Soup Nazi," episode 116, dir. Andy Ackerman, writer Spike Feresten, perf. Jerry Seinfeld, Jason Alexander, Julia Louis-Dreyfus, Michael Richards, Alexandra Wentworth, Larry Thomas, NBC, November 2, 1995.

	Short note	[99] *Seinfeld*, "Soup Nazi."
	Bibliography	*Seinfeld*, "The Soup Nazi." Episode 116. Dir. Andy Ackerman. Writer Spike Feresten. Perf. Jerry Seinfeld, Jason Alexander, Julia Louis-Dreyfus, Michael Richards, Alexandra Wentworth, Larry Thomas. NBC, November 2, 1995.

Film	First note	[99] *Godfather II.* DVD, dir. Francis Ford Coppola (1974; Los Angeles: Paramount Home Video, 2003).

▶ If you wish to cite individual scenes, which are accessible on DVDs, treat them like chapters in books. "Murder of Fredo," *Godfather II* . . .

	Short note	[99] *Godfather II.*
	Bibliography	*Godfather II.* DVD. Dir. Francis Ford Coppola. Perf. Al Pacino, Robert De Niro, Robert Duvall, Diane Keaton. Screenplay by Francis Ford Coppola and Mario Puzo based on novel by Mario Puzo. 1974; Paramount Home Video, 2003.

Film (*continued*)		▸ Title, director, studio, and year of release are all required. So is the year the video recording was released, if that's what you are citing. ▸ Optional: the actors, producers, screenwriters, editors, cinematographers, and other information. You can include what you need for your paper, in order of their importance to your analysis. Their names appear between the title and the distributor.
Artwork, original	First note	[99]Jacopo Robusti Tintoretto, *The Birth of John the Baptist*, 1550s, Hermitage, St. Petersburg. ▸ The year of the painting is optional.
	Short note	[99]Tintoretto, *Birth of John the Baptist*.
	Bibliography	Tintoretto, Jacopo Robusti. *The Birth of John the Baptist*. 1550s. Hermitage, St. Petersburg.
Artwork, reproduction	First note	[99]Jacopo Robusti Tintoretto, *The Birth of John the Baptist*, 1550s, in Tom Nichols, *Tintoretto: Tradition and Identity* (London: Reaktion Books, 1999), 47.
	Short note	[99]Tintoretto, *The Birth of John the Baptist*.
	Bibliography	Tintoretto, Jacopo Robusti. *The Birth of John the Baptist*. 1550s. In Tom Nichols, *Tintoretto: Tradition and Identity*, 47. London: Reaktion Books, 1999.
Artwork, online	First note	[99]Jacopo Robusti Tintoretto, *The Birth of John the Baptist*, 1550s, Hermitage, St. Petersburg, http://www.hermitage.ru/html_En/index.html (accessed February 1, 2004). [99]Jacopo Robusti Tintoretto, *The Birth of John the Baptist* (detail), 1550s, Hermitage, St. Petersburg. http://cgfa.floridaimaging.com/t/p-tintore1.htm (accessed January 6, 2004).
	Short note	[99]Tintoretto, *The Birth of John the Baptist*.
	Bibliography	Tintoretto, Jacopo Robusti. *The Birth of John the Baptist*. 1550s. Hermitage, St. Petersburg. http://www.hermitage.ru/html_En/index.html (accessed February 1, 2004).

Tintoretto, Jacopo Robusti. *The Birth of John the Baptist* (detail). 1550s. Hermitage, St. Petersburg. http://cgfa.floridaimaging.com/t/p-tintore1.htm (accessed January 6, 2004).

Photograph	First note	[99]Ansel Adams, *Monolith, the Face of Half Dome, Yosemite National Park*, 1927, Art Institute, Chicago.
	Short note	[99]Adams, *Monolith*.
	Bibliography	Adams, Ansel. *Monolith, the Face of Half Dome, Yosemite National Park*. 1927. Art Institute, Chicago.
Figures: map, chart, graph, or table	First citation	▶ Citation for a map, chart, graph, or table normally appears as a credit below the item rather than as a footnote or endnote. *Source:* Daryl G. Press, "The Myth of Air Power in the Persian Gulf War and the Future of Warfare," *International Security* 26 (Fall 2001): 17, fig. 2. *Source:* http://www.usatoday.com/news/vote2000/cbc/map.htm (accessed August 30, 2004). *Source:* Topographic Maps (California), National Geographic Society, 2004, http://mapmachine.nationalgeographic.com/mapmachine/viewandcustomize.html?task=getMap&themeId =113&size=s&state=zoomBox (accessed August 30, 2004).
	Short citation	*Source:* Press, "Myth of Air Power," 17, fig. 2.
	Bibliography	Press, Daryl G. "The Myth of Air Power in the Persian Gulf War and the Future of Warfare." *International Security* 26 (Fall 2001): 5–44. Electoral Vote Map [2000]. http://www.usatoday.com/news/vote2000/cbc/map.htm (accessed August 30, 2004). Topographic Maps (California). National Geographic Society. 2004. http://mapmachine.nationalgeographic.com/

Figures (*continued*)		mapmachine/viewandcustomize.html?task= getMap&themeId=113&size=s&state= zoomBox (accessed August 30, 2004).
Musical recording	First note	[99]Robert Johnson, "Cross Road Blues," 1937, *Robert Johnson: King of the Delta Blues Singers* (Columbia Records 1654, 1961). [99]Samuel Barber, "Cello Sonata, for cello and piano, Op. 6," *Barber: Adagio for Strings, Violin Concerto, Orchestral and Chamber Works*, disc 2, St. Louis Symphony, Leonard Slatkin, cond.; Alan Stepansky, cello; Israela Margalit, piano (EMI Classics 74287, 2001).
	Short note	[99]Johnson, "Cross Road Blues." [99]Barber, "Cello Sonata, Op. 6."
	Bibliography	Johnson, Robert. "Cross Road Blues." *Robert Johnson: King of the Delta Blues Singers*. Columbia Records 1654, 1961. Barber, Samuel. "Cello Sonata, for cello and piano, Op. 6." *Barber: Adagio for Strings, Violin Concerto, Orchestral and Chamber Works*. Disc 2, St. Louis Symphony. Leonard Slatkin, cond.; Alan Stepansky, cello; Israela Margalit, piano. EMI Classics 74287, 2001.
Sheet music	First note	[99]Johann Sebastian Bach, "Toccata and Fugue in D Minor," 1708, BWV 565, arr. Ferruccio Benvenuto Busoni for solo piano (New York: G. Schirmer, LB1629, 1942).
	Short note	[99]Bach, "Toccata and Fugue in D Minor."
	Bibliography	Bach, Johann Sebastian. "Toccata and Fugue in D Minor." 1708. BWV 565. Arr. Ferruccio Benvenuto Busoni for solo piano. New York: G. Schirmer LB1629, 1942.

▶ This piece was written in 1708 and has the standard Bach classification BWV 565. This particular arrangement was published by G. Schirmer in 1942 and has their catalog number LB1629.

Liner notes	First note	[99]Steven Reich, liner notes for *Different Trains* (Elektra/Nonesuch 9 79176-2, 1988).
	Short note	[99]Reich, liner notes.
		▸ Or
		[99]Reich, liner notes, *Different Trains*.
	Bibliography	Reich, Steven. Liner notes for *Different Trains*. Elektra/Nonesuch 9 79176-2, 1988.

Government document, hard copy and online	First note	[99]Senate Committee on Armed Services, *Hearings on S. 758, A Bill to Promote the National Security by Providing for a National Defense Establishment*, 80th Cong., 1st sess., 1947, S. Rep. 239, 13.
		▸ "S. Rep. 239, 13" refers to report number 239, page 13.
		[99]Environmental Protection Agency (EPA), *Final Rule, Air Pollution Control: Prevention of Significant Deterioration; Approval and Promulgation of Implementation Plans*, *Federal Register* 68, no. 247 (December 24, 2003): 74483–91.
		[99]United States, Department of State. "China—25th Anniversary of Diplomatic Relations," press statement, December 31, 2003, http://www.state.gov/r/pa/prs/ps/2003/27632.htm (accessed March 15, 2004).
	Short note	[99]Senate, *Hearings on S. 758*, 13.
		[99]EPA, *Final Rule, Air Pollution Control*.
		[99]State Department, "China—25th Anniversary."
	Bibliography	U.S. Congress. Senate. Committee on Armed Services. *Hearings on S. 758, Bill to Promote the National Security by Providing for a National Defense Establishment*. 80th Cong., 1st sess., 1947. S. Rep. 239.
		Environmental Protection Agency. *Final Rule, Air Pollution Control: Prevention of Significant Deterioration; Approval and Promulgation of Implementation Plans*. *Federal Register* 68, no. 247 (December 24, 2003): 74483–91.

Government document (*continued*)		United States, Department of State. "China—25th Anniversary of Diplomatic Relations," press statement, December 31, 2003. http://www.state.gov/r/pa/prs/ps/ 2003/27632.htm.
Software	First note	[99]*Stata 8* (for Linux 64) (College Station, TX: Stata, 2003). [99]*Dreamweaver MX 2004* (San Francisco: Macromedia, 2003).
	Short note	[99]*Stata 8* (for Linux 64). [99]*Dreamweaver MX 2004*.
	Bibliography	*Stata 8* (for Linux 64). College Station, TX: Stata, 2003. *Dreamweaver MX 2004*. San Francisco: Macromedia, 2003.
Database	First note	[99]*Corpus Scriptorum Latinorum* database of Latin literature, http://www.forumromanum .org/literature/index.html.

▸ For a specific item within this database:

[99]Gaius Julius Caesar, *Commentarii de bello civili*, ed. A. G. Peskett (Loeb Classical Library; London: W. Heinemann, 1914), in *Corpus Scriptorum Latinorum* database of Latin literature, http://www.thelatinlibrary.com/ caes.html.

[99]*Intellectual Property Treaties*, *InterAm Database* (Tucson, AZ: National Law Center for Inter-American Free Trade), http://www .natlaw.com/database.htm (accessed January 10, 2004).

▸ For a specific item within this database:

[99]"Chile-U.S. Free Trade Agreement (June 6, 2003)," in *Intellectual Property Treaties*, *InterAm Database* (Tucson, AZ: National Law Center for Inter-American Free Trade), http://www.natlaw .com/treaties/chileusfta.htm (accessed January 12, 2004).

Short note	[99]*Corpus Scriptorum Latinorum.* [99]*Intellectual Property Treaties, InterAm Database.* [99]"Chile-U.S. Free Trade Agreement."
Bibliography	*Corpus Scriptorum Latinorum.* Database of Latin literature. http://www.forumromanum.org/literature/index.html. Caesar, Gaius Julius. *Commentarii de bello civili.* Edited by A. G. Peskett. Loeb Classical Library. London: W. Heinemann, 1914. In *Corpus Scriptorum Latinorum* database of Latin literature. http://www.thelatinlibrary.com/caes.html. *Intellectual Property Treaties, InterAm Database.* Tucson, AZ: National Law Center for Inter-American Free Trade. http://www.natlaw.com/database.htm (accessed January 10, 2004).

▶ For a specific item within the database:

"Chile-U.S. Free Trade Agreement (June 6, 2003)." In *Intellectual Property Treaties, InterAm Database.* Tucson, AZ: National Law Center for Inter-American Free Trade. http://www.natlaw.com/treaties/chileusfta.htm (accessed January 12, 2004).

Web site, entire	First note	[99]Digital History Web site, ed. Steven Mintz, http://www.digitalhistory.uh.edu/index.cfm?. [99]Internet Public Library (IPL), http://www.ipl.org/. [99]Yale University, History Department home page, http://www.yale.edu/history/.

▶ You may omit "home page" if it is obvious.

	Short note	[99]Digital History Web site. [99]Internet Public Library. [99]Yale History Department home page.
	Bibliography	Digital History Web site. Edited by Steven Mintz. http://www.digitalhistory.uh.edu/index.cfm?. Internet Public Library (IPL). http://www.ipl.org/.

Web site (*continued*)		Yale University. History Department home page. http://www.yale.edu/history/.
Web page, with author	First note	[99]Charles Lipson, "Scholarly Tools Online to Study World Politics," http://www.charleslipson.com/scholarly-links.htm.
	Short note	[99]Lipson, "Scholarly Tools."
	Bibliography	Lipson, Charles. "Scholarly Tools Online to Study World Politics." http://www.charleslipson.com/scholarly-links.htm.
		▸ Include the title or description of the Web page if available. That way, if the link changes, it may still be possible to find the page through a search.
Web page, no author	First note	[99]"*I Love Lucy*: Series Summary," *Sitcoms Online*, http://www.sitcomsonline.com/ilovelucy.html (accessed May 4, 2005).
	Short note	[99] "*I Love Lucy*: Series Summary."
	Bibliography	"*I Love Lucy*: Series Summary." *Sitcoms Online*. http://www.sitcomsonline.com/ilovelucy.html (accessed May 4, 2005).
Weblog entry or comment	First note	[99]Daniel Drezner, "Blogger Weirdness," *Daniel W. Drezner* Weblog, entry posted December 30, 2003, http://www.danieldrezner.com/blog/ (accessed March 14, 2004). [99]Tyler Cowen, "Trial by Jury," *Volokh Conspiracy* Weblog, entry posted December 30, 2003, http://volokh.com/ (accessed January 6, 2004). [99]Kiwi (Janice Walker), "Citing Weblogs," *Kairosnews: A Weblog for Discussing Rhetoric, Technology, and Pedagogy*, comment posted December 13, 2003, http://kairosnews.org/node/view/3542 (accessed December 28, 2003). [99]Josh Chafetz, untitled Weblog entry, *OxBlog* Weblog, posted 12:06 p.m., December 27, 2003, http://oxblog.blogspot.com/ (accessed December 31, 2003).

	Short note	⁹⁹Drezner, "Blogger Weirdness." ⁹⁹Cowen, "Trial by Jury." ⁹⁹Kiwi (Janice Walker), "Citing Weblogs." ⁹⁹Chafetz, untitled Weblog entry, December 27, 2003.

Short note: ⁹⁹Drezner, "Blogger Weirdness."
⁹⁹Cowen, "Trial by Jury."
⁹⁹Kiwi (Janice Walker), "Citing Weblogs."
⁹⁹Chafetz, untitled Weblog entry, December 27, 2003.

Bibliography: Drezner, Daniel. "Blogger Weirdness." *Daniel W. Drezner* Weblog. Entry posted December 30, 2003. http://www.danieldrezner.com/blog/ (accessed March 14, 2004).

Cowen, Tyler. "Trial by Jury." *Volokh Conspiracy* Weblog. Entry posted December 24, 2003. http://volokh.com/ (accessed January 6, 2004).

Kiwi (Janice Walker). "Citing Weblogs." *Kairosnews: A Weblog for Discussing Rhetoric, Technology, and Pedagogy.* Weblog comment posted December 13, 2003, to http://kairosnews.org/node/view/3542 (accessed December 28, 2003).

Chafetz, Josh. [Untitled Weblog entry.] *OxBlog.* Entry posted 12:06 p.m., December 27, 2003. http://oxblog.blogspot.com/ (accessed December 31, 2003).

▶ Chafetz's posting had no title and is one of several he posted the same day to this group blog. Listing the time identifies it.

E-mail or electronic newsgroup

First note: ⁹⁹Chicago Council on Foreign Relations, "Blending Islam and Democracy: Southeast Asia's Unique Experience," *e-Chronicle*, May 2005 edition, e-mail to Chicago Council on Foreign Relations mailing list, April 27, 2005, http://www.ccfr.org/publications/pdf/may05.pdf.

⁹⁹Eva Wilhelm, e-mail to Nicholson Center for British Studies, University of Chicago, mailing list, April 27, 2005.

▶ Include the URL if the mass e-mailing has been archived.

⁹⁹ Kathy Leis, e-mail message to author, May 7, 2005.

| E-mail or electronic newsgroup (*continued*) | Short note | [99]Chicago Council on Foreign Relations, "Blending Islam and Democracy," April 27, 2005. [99]Eva Wilhelm, e-mail to Nicholson Center for British Studies, University of Chicago, April 27, 2005. [99] Kathy Leis, e-mail message to author, May 7, 2005. |
| | Bibliography | ▸ Personal e-mails, such as the one above from Kathy Leis, and non-archived discussion groups are not included in the bibliography because they cannot be retrieved by third parties. You should include newsgroups, Listservs, and archived discussions if they can be accessed; include the URL for them.

Chicago Council on Foreign Relations. "Blending Islam and Democracy: Southeast Asia's Unique Experience." *e-Chronicle*, May 2005 edition, e-mail to Chicago Council on Foreign Relations mailing list, April 27, 2005. http://www.ccfr.org/publications/pdf/may05.pdf. |

CHICAGO: CITATIONS TO TABLES AND NOTES

Citation	Refers to
106	page 106
106n	only note appearing on page 106
107 n. 32	note number 32 on page 107, a page with several notes
89, table 6.2	table 6.2, which appears on page 89; similar for graphs and figures

CHICAGO: COMMON ABBREVIATIONS IN CITATIONS

and others	et al.	editor	ed.	page	p.
appendix	app.	especially	esp.	pages	pp.
book	bk.	figure	fig.	part	pt.
chapter	chap.	note	n.	pseudonym	pseud.
compare	cf.	notes	nn.	translator	trans.
document	doc.	number	no.	versus	vs.
edition	ed.	opus	op.	volume	vol.

Note: All abbreviations are lowercase, followed by a period. Most form their plurals by adding "s." The exceptions are note (n. → nn.), opus (op. → opp.), page (p. → pp.), and translator (same abbreviation).

In citing poetry, do not use abbreviations for "line" or "lines" since a lowercase "l" is easily confused with the number one.

FAQS ABOUT CHICAGO-STYLE CITATIONS

Why do you put the state after some publishers and not after others?
The Chicago Manual of Style recommends using state names for all but the largest, best-known cities. To avoid confusion, they use Cambridge, MA, for Harvard and MIT presses but just Cambridge for Cambridge University Press in the ancient English university town. Also, you can drop the state name if it is already included in the publisher's title, such as Ann Arbor: University of Michigan Press.

What if a book is forthcoming?
Use "forthcoming" just as you would use the year. Here's a bibliographic entry:

Godot, Shlomo. *Still Waiting.* London: Verso, forthcoming.

What if the date or place of publication is missing?
Same idea as "forthcoming." Where you would normally put the place or date, use "n.p." (no place) or "n.d." (no date). For example: (Montreal, QC: McGill-Queen's University Press, n.d.).

What if the author is anonymous or not listed?
Usually, you omit the anonymous author and begin with the title.

If an author is technically anonymous but is actually known, put the name in brackets, as in [Johnson, Samuel] or [Madison, James] and list it wherever the author's name falls.

One book I cite has a title that ends with a question mark. Do I still put periods or commas after it?
No.

Are notes single-spaced or double-spaced? What about the bibliography?
Space your footnotes and endnotes the same way you do your text.

As for your bibliography, I think it is easiest to read if you single space within entries and put a double space between the entries. But check what your department or publisher wants. They may require double spacing for everything.

I'm reading Mark Twain. Do I cite Twain or Samuel Clemens?
When pseudonyms are well known such as Mark Twain or Mother Teresa, you can use them alone, without explanation, if you wish.

If you want to include both the pseudonym and the given name, the rule is simple. Put the better-known name first, followed by the lesser-known one in brackets. It doesn't matter if the "real" name is the lesser-known one.

George Eliot [Mary Ann Evans]
Isak Dinesen [Karen Christence Dinesen, Baroness Blixen-Finecke]
Le Corbusier [Charles-Edouard Jeanneret]
Benjamin Disraeli [Lord Beaconsfield]
Lord Palmerston [Henry John Temple]
Krusty the Clown [Herschel S. Krustofski]

If you wish to include the pseudonym in a bibliographic entry, it reads:

Aleichem, Sholom [Solomon Rabinovitz]. *Fiddler on the Roof...*

4 MLA CITATIONS FOR THE HUMANITIES

The Modern Language Association (MLA) has developed a citation style that is widely used in the humanities. Instead of footnotes or endnotes, it uses in-text citations such as (Strier 125). Full information about each item appears in the bibliography, which MLA calls "Works Cited." Like other bibliographies, it contains three essential nuggets of information about each item: the author, title, and publication data. To illustrate, let's use a book by Fouad Ajami. The full entry in the Works Cited is

> Ajami, Fouad. The Dream Palace of the Arabs: A Generation's Odyssey. New York: Pantheon, 1998.

Titles are underlined rather than italicized.

In-text citations are brief and simple. To cite the entire book, just insert (Ajami) at the end of the sentence, or (Ajami 12) to refer to page 12. If your paper happens to cite several books by Ajami, be sure your reader knows which one you are referring to. If that's not clear in the sentence, then include a very brief title: (Ajami, Dream 12).

MLA citations can be even briefer—and they should be, whenever possible. They can omit the author and the title as long as it's clear which work is being cited. For example:

> As Ajami notes, these are long-standing problems in Arab intellectual life (14–33).

You can omit the in-text reference entirely if the author and title are clear and you are not citing specific pages. For instance:

> Gibbon's Decline and Fall of the Roman Empire established new standards of documentary evidence for historians.

In this case, there's nothing to put in an in-text reference that isn't already in the sentence. So, given MLA's consistent emphasis on brevity, you simply skip the reference. You still include Gibbon in your Works Cited.

Because in-text references are so brief, you can string several together in one parenthesis: (Bevington 17; Bloom 75; Vendler 51). The authors' names are separated by semicolons.

If Ajami's book were a three-volume work, then the citation to volume 3, page 17, would be (Ajami 3: 17). If you need to differentiate this work from others by the same author, then include the title: (Ajami, Dream 3: 17). If you wanted to cite the volume but not a specific page, then use (Ajami, vol. 3) or (Ajami, Dream, vol. 3). Why include "vol." here? So readers won't think you are citing page 3 of a one-volume work.

If several authors have the same last name, simply add their first initials to differentiate them: (C. Brontë, Jane Eyre), (E. Brontë, Wuthering Heights). Of course, full information about the authors and their works appears at the end, in the Works Cited.

Books like *Jane Eyre* appear in countless editions, and your readers may wish to look up passages in theirs. To make that easier, the MLA recommends that you add some information after the normal page citation. You might say, for example, that the passage appears in chapter 1. For poems, you would note the verse and lines.

Let's say that you quoted a passage from the first chapter of *Jane Eyre*, which appeared on page 7 in the edition you are using. Insert a semicolon after the page and add the chapter number, using a lowercase abbreviation for chapter: (E. Brontë, Wuthering Heights 7; ch. 1). For plays, the act, scene, and lines are separated by periods (Romeo and Juliet 1.3.12–15).

When you refer to online documents, there are often no pages to cite. As a substitute, include a section or paragraph number, if there is one. Just put a comma after the author's name, then list the section or paragraph: (Padgett, sec. 9.7) or (Snidal, pars. 12–18). If there's no numbering system, just list the author. Don't cite your printout because those pages vary from person to person, printer to printer.[1]

In-text citations normally appear at the end of sentences and are followed by the punctuation for the sentence itself. To illustrate:

A full discussion of these citation issues appears in the MLA Handbook (Gibaldi).

---

1. These recommendations follow the MLA's own recommendation. MLA, "Frequently Asked Questions about MLA Style," http://www.mla.org/publications/style/style_faq/style_faq7.

In this style, you can still use regular footnotes or endnotes for limited purposes. They can *only* be used for commentary, however, not for citations. If you need to cite some materials within the note itself, use in-text citations there, just as you would in the text.

For brevity—a paramount virtue of the MLA system—the names of publishers are also compressed: Princeton University Press becomes Princeton UP, the University of Chicago Press becomes U of Chicago P. For the same reason, most month names are abbreviated.

MLA throws brevity overboard, however, when referencing electronic information. If the works were originally printed, the Works Cited include all the print information, plus some extra information about the online versions, including Web sites, sponsoring organizations, access dates, and URLs. Of all citation styles, only MLA requires listing the sponsoring organization. This leads to redundancy. You are supposed to write: Encyclopaedia Britannica Online. 2004. Encyclopaedia Britannica . . . Or CBSNews.com. 5 Jan. 2004. CBS . . . The underlined titles are the works cited; the repeated name is the sponsoring organization. Actually, we'll see the name a third time in the URL, <http://www.cbs.com>. This seems like overkill to me, at least when the sponsoring organization is evident. But that's the current MLA style.

If an item is exclusively online, like a Web page or Weblog, the citation includes the author, the title of the Web page or site, the date it was created (or updated), plus information about the Web site, sponsoring organization, the date it was accessed, and the URL. It makes for a long list.

I have provided detailed information and examples in a table below. Because MLA style is often used in the humanities, where citations to plays, poems, paintings, and films are common, I include all of them. If you want still more examples or less common items, consult two useful books published by the MLA:

- Joseph Gibaldi, *MLA Style Manual and Guide to Scholarly Publishing,* 2nd ed. (New York: Modern Language Association of America, 1998), 149–254.
- Joseph Gibaldi, *MLA Handbook for Writers of Research Papers,* 6th ed. (New York: Modern Language Association of America, 2003).

They should be available in your library's reference section.

To make it easy to find the MLA citations you need, I've listed them here alphabetically, along with the pages where they are described.

INDEX OF MLA CITATIONS IN THIS CHAPTER

MLA: WORKS CITED AND IN-TEXT CITATIONS

Book, one author	Works Cited	Lipson, Charles. Reliable Partners: How Democracies Have Made a Separate Peace. Princeton: Princeton UP, 2003.
		Reed, Christopher A. Gutenberg in Shanghai: Chinese Print Capitalism, 1876–1937. Vancouver: U British Columbia P, 2004.

▶ MLA style omits the publisher's state or province.

	In-text	(Lipson, <u>Reliable</u> 22–23) or (Lipson 22–23) or (22–23) ▸ Refers to pages 22 23. (Reed, <u>Gutenberg</u> 136) or (Reed 136) or (136)
Books, several by same author	Works Cited	Weinberg, Gerhard L. <u>Germany, Hitler, and World War II: Essays in Modern German and World History</u>. Cambridge: Cambridge UP, 1995. ---. <u>A World at Arms: A Global History of World War II</u>. Cambridge: Cambridge UP, 1994. ▸ The repetition of the author's name uses three hyphens, followed by a period.
	In-text	(Weinberg, <u>Germany</u> 34; Weinberg, <u>World</u> 456)
Book, multiple authors	Works Cited	Binder, Guyora, and Robert Weisberg. <u>Literary Criticisms of Law</u>. Princeton: Princeton UP, 2000. ▸ If four or more authors: Binder, Guyora, et al.
	In-text	(Binder and Weisberg, <u>Literary Criticisms</u> 15–26) or (Binder and Weisberg 15–26)
Book, multiple editions	Works Cited	Strunk, William, Jr., and E. B. White. <u>The Elements of Style</u>. 4th ed. New York: Longman, 2000. ▸ If this were a multivolume work, then the volume number would come after the edition: 4th ed. Vol. 2.
	In-text	(Strunk and White, <u>Elements</u> 12) or (Strunk and White 12)
Book, edited	Works Cited	Robinson, Francis, ed. <u>Cambridge Illustrated History of the Islamic World</u>. Cambridge: Cambridge UP, 1996. Gallagher, Kathleen, and David Booth, eds. <u>How Theatre Educates: Convergences and Counterpoints with Artists, Scholars, and Advocates</u>. Toronto: U Toronto P, 2003.

	In-text	(Robinson)
		(Gallagher and Booth)

Book, anonymous or no author	Works Cited	Through Our Enemies' Eyes: Osama Bin Laden, Radical Islam, and the Future of America. Washington, DC: Brassey's, 2003.
		Golden Verses of the Pythagoreans. Whitefish, MT: Kessinger, 2003.
		▸ Do not use "anonymous" as the author. If the author is unknown, alphabetize by title but ignore any initial article ("a," "an," or "the"). So, The Holy Koran is alphabetized under "H."
	In-text	(Through Our Enemies' Eyes)
		(Golden Verses)

Book, online	Works Cited	Dickens, Charles. Great Expectations. 1860–61. Project Gutenberg Archive. Etext 1400. 14 Jan. 2004 ‹http://www.gutenberg.net/etext98/grexp10.txt›.
		▸ The date when you access the online content (in this case, 14 Jan. 2004) comes immediately before the URL. Notice that the day comes before the month; that's standard with MLA. There is no punctuation between this date and the URL.[2]
	In-text	(Dickens)
		▸ Since this electronic version does not have pagination, cite the chapter numbers.
		(Dickens, ch. 2)

Multivolume work	Works Cited	Pflanze, Otto. Bismarck and the Development of Germany. 3 vols. Princeton: Princeton UP, 1963–90.

---

2. This follows the MLA's most recent recommendation: http://www.mla.org/publications/style/style_faq/style_faq4.

	In-text	(Pflanze) or (Pflanze 3: 21) ▸ This refers to volume 3, page 21. (Pflanze, vol. 3) ▸ When a volume is referenced without a specific page, then use "vol." so the volume won't be confused for a page number.
Single volume in a multivolume work	Works Cited	Pflanze, Otto. <u>The Period of Fortification, 1880–1898</u>. Princeton: Princeton UP, 1990. Vol. 3 of <u>Bismarck and the Development of Germany</u>. 3 vols. 1963–90. Iriye, Akira. <u>The Globalizing of America</u>. Cambridge: Cambridge UP, 1993. Vol. 3 of <u>Cambridge History of American Foreign Relations</u>, ed. Warren I. Cohen. 4 vols. 1993.
	In-text	(Pflanze) (Iriye)
Reprint of earlier edition	Works Cited	Barzun, Jacques. <u>Simple and Direct: A Rhetoric for Writers</u>. 1985. Chicago: U of Chicago P, 1994. Smith, Adam. <u>An Inquiry into the Nature and Causes of the Wealth of Nations</u>. 1776. Ed. Edwin Cannan. Chicago: U of Chicago P, 1976.
	In-text	(Barzun, <u>Simple</u>) or (Barzun) (Smith, <u>Wealth of Nations</u>) or (Smith)
Translated volume	Works Cited	Weber, Max. <u>The Protestant Ethic and the Spirit of Capitalism</u>. 1904–5. Trans. Talcott Parsons. New York: Charles Scribner's Sons, 1958. Tocqueville, Alexis de. <u>Democracy in America</u>. Ed. J. P. Mayer. Trans. George Lawrence. New York: HarperCollins, 2000. ▸ Editor and translator are listed in the order in which they appear on the book's title page.

Translated volume (*continued*)		Beowulf: A New Verse Translation. Trans. Seamus Heaney. New York: Farrar, Straus and Giroux, 2000.
		▸ *Beowulf* is an anonymous poem. The translator's name normally comes after the title. But there is an exception. If you wish to comment on the translator's work, then place the translator's name first. For example:
		Heaney, Seamus, trans. Beowulf: A New Verse Translation. New York: Farrar, Straus and Giroux, 2000.
		Parsons, Talcott, trans. The Protestant Ethic and the Spirit of Capitalism, by Max Weber. 1904–5. New York: Charles Scribner's Sons, 1958.
	In-text	(Weber, Protestant Ethic) or (Weber) (Tocqueville, Democracy in America) or (Tocqueville) (Heaney, Beowulf) or (Beowulf) (Parsons)
Chapter in edited book	Works Cited	Keohane, Robert. "The Demand for International Regimes." In International Regimes, ed. Stephen Krasner. Ithaca: Cornell UP, 1983. 56–67.
	In-text	(Keohane 56–67)
Journal article, one author	Works Cited	Kleppinger, Stanley V. "On the Influence of Jazz Rhythm in the Music of Aaron Copland." American Music 21.1 (Spring 2003): 74–111.
		▸ Refers to volume 21, number 1.
		▸ The issue number is optional if it is clear how to find the article (perhaps because you have already included the month or because the pages run continuously through the year). But if each issue begins with page 1 and you include only the year, then you need to add the issue number or month to show where the article appears: American Music 21.1 (2003): 74–111.

	In-text	(Kleppinger) or (Kleppinger 74–82) or (Kleppinger, "Aaron Copland" 74–82)
		▸ The title may be needed to differentiate this article from others by the same author.
Journal article, multiple authors	Works Cited	Koremenos, Barbara, Charles Lipson, and Duncan Snidal. "The Rational Design of International Institutions." International Organization 55 (Autumn 2001): 761–99.
		▸ If there are four or more authors: Koremenos, Barbara, et al.
	In-text	(Koremenos, Lipson, and Snidal 761–99)
Journal article, online	Works Cited	Small, Christopher. "Why Doesn't the Whole World Love Chamber Music?" American Music 19.3 (Autumn 2001): 340–59. JSTOR 15 Mar. 2004 ‹http://www.jstor.org/search›.
		▸ This is a normal print journal, available online from multiple sources, with the same pagination as the print version. Here I list it through JSTOR. The URL is quite long, so MLA recommends listing only the search page.
		North, Dan. "Magic and Illusion in Early Cinema." Studies in French Cinema 1.2 (2001): 70–79. EBSCOhost Research Database 6 Jan. 2004 ‹http://search.epnet. com›.
	In-text	(Small) or (Small 341–43) or (Small, "Chamber Music" 341–43) (North) or (North 70–79) or (North, "Magic" 70–79)
Journal article, foreign language	Works Cited	Ma'oz, Zvi Uri. "Y a-t-il des juifs sans synagogue?" Revue des Études Juives 163 (2004): 483–93.
	In-text	(Ma'oz) or (Ma'oz 492)

Newspaper or magazine article, no author	Works Cited	"Report of 9/11 Panel Cites Lapses by C.I.A. and F.B.I." <u>New York Times</u> 23 July 2003: 1. ▸ This refers to page 1.
	In-text	("Report of 9/11 Panel" 1)
Newspaper or magazine article, with author	Works Cited	Bruni, Frank. "Pope Pleads for End to Terrorism and War." <u>New York Times</u> 26 Dec. 2003, national ed.: A21. ▸ It's always fine to include the headline and reporter's name. The MLA says you can omit them, though, if they do not add to the point you are making in the text.
	In-text	(Bruni A21)
Newspaper or magazine article, online	Works Cited	"European Unity: The History of an Idea." <u>The Economist</u> 30 Dec. 2003. 6 Jan. 2004 ‹http://www.economist.com/world/europe/displayStory.cfm?story_id=2313040›. ▸ The first date refers to the article, the second to the day it was accessed. ▸ For magazines and newspapers, there is no need to reference the sponsoring organization. Salamon, Julie. "Collaborating on the Future at the Modern." <u>New York Times</u> 26 Dec. 2003. 2 Jan. 2004 ‹http://www.nytimes.com/2003/12/26/arts/design/26CURA.html›.
	In-text	("European Unity") (Salamon) or (Salamon, "Collaborating") if you cite more than one article by this author.
Review	Works Cited	Orr, H. Allen. "What's Not in Your Genes." Rev. of <u>Nature via Nurture: Genes, Experience, and What Makes Us Human</u>, by Matt Ridley. <u>New York Review of Books</u> 50 (14 Aug. 2003): 38–40.
	In-text	(Orr) or (Orr, "Genes")

Unpublished paper, thesis, or dissertation	Works Cited	Nishi, Takayushi. "The Humiliating Gift: Negative Reactions to International Help." Paper presented at the Program on International Politics, Economics, and Security, U Chicago. 4 Mar. 2004. Besser-Jones, Lorraine. "The Moral Commitment to Public Reason." MA thesis. Claremont Graduate School, 1997. Pérez-Torres, Rafael. "Screen Play and Inscription: Narrative Strategies in Four Post-1960s Novels." Diss. Stanford, 1989.
	In-text	(Nishi 1–35) (Besser-Jones) (Pérez-Torres)
Abstract	Works Cited	Lambe, J. L. "Who Wants to Censor Pornography and Hate Speech?" Mass Communications and Society 7 (2004): 279–99. Communication Abstracts 28 (Feb. 2005): 25–26, item 0051. Cheetham, Mark A., Michael Ann Holly, and Keith Moxey. "Visual Studies, Historiography and Aesthetics." Journal of Visual Culture 4 (Apr. 2005): 75–90. Abstract. <http://www.swetswise.com/eAccess/viewAbstract.do?articleID+23067302&assn+4670628>.
	In-text	(Lambe) (Cheetham, Holley, and Moxey)
Microfilm, microfiche	Works Cited	Abbott, Alice Irving. Circumstantial Evidence. New York: W. B. Smith, 1882. In American Fiction, 1774–1910. Reel A-1. Woodbridge: Gale/Primary Source Microfilm, 1998. King, Martin Luther, Jr., FBI file [microform]. Ed. David J. Garrow. 16 reels. Frederick: U Publications of Am, 1984.

Microfilm *(continued)*	In-text	(Abbott) To cite page 13 on reel A-1, use (Abbott A-1: 13) (King) To cite reel 2, page 12, use (King 2: 12)

Archival materials and manuscript collections, hard copies and online	Works Cited	Franklin, Isaac. Letter to R. C. Ballard. 28 Feb. 1831. Series 1.1, folder 1. Rice Ballard Papers. Southern Historical Collection. Wilson Lib. U of North Carolina, Chapel Hill. Lamson, Mary Swift. An Account of the Beginning of the B.Y.W.C.A. Ms. Boston YWCA Papers. Schlesinger Lib. Radcliffe Institute for Advanced Study, Harvard U. Cambridge, MA. 1891. ▸ Manuscript is abbreviated ms. Typescript is "ts." Spell out "notebook" and "unpublished essay." Szold, Henrietta. Letter to Rose Jacobs. 3 Feb. 1932. Reel 1, book 1. Rose Jacobs–Alice L. Seligsberg Collection. Judaica Microforms. Brandeis Lib. Waltham, MA. Szold, Henrietta. Letter to Rose Jacobs. 9 Mar. 1936. A/125/112. Central Zionist Archives, Jerusalem. Taraval, Sigismundo. Journal Recounting Indian Uprisings in Baja California. Handwritten ms. 1734–1737. Edward E. Ayer Manuscript Collection No. 1240, Newberry Lib. Chicago, IL. Taft, Horatio Nelson. Diary. Vol. 1, Jan. 1, 1861–April 11, 1862. Manuscript Division, Lib. of Congress. 30 May 2004 ‹http://memory.loc.gov/cgi-bin/ampage?collId=mtaft&fileName=mtaft1/mtaftmtaft1.db&recNum=148›.
	In-text	(Franklin) or (Franklin to Ballard) or (Franklin to Ballard, 28 Feb. 1831) (Lamson) or (Lamson 2) (Szold) or (Szold to Jacobs) or (Szold to Jacobs, 3 Feb. 1932)

(Szold) or (Szold to Jacobs) or (Szold to Jacobs, 9 Mar. 1936)

(Taraval) or (Taraval ¶ 23)

▸ This manuscript uses paragraph numbers, not pages

(Taft) or (Taft 149)

Encyclopedia, hard copy and online	Works Cited	"African Arts." Encyclopaedia Britannica. 15th ed. 1987. 13: 134–80. ▸ Alphabetize by the first significant word in title. ▸ Volume and page numbers are optional. ▸ Edition and year are required, but you can omit the city and publisher for well-known encyclopedias, dictionaries, and other references. "Art, African." Encyclopaedia Britannica Online. 2004. Encyclopaedia Britannica. 5 Jan. 2004 ‹http://search.eb.com/eb/article?eu= 119483›. ▸ Why does the name, *Encyclopaedia Britannica*, appear twice? Because it is both the publication and the "sponsoring organization," and MLA rules currently require that you list both. Chanda, Jacqueline. "African Art and Architecture," Microsoft Encarta Online Encyclopedia. 2004. Microsoft Corporation. 7 Jan. 2004 ‹http://encarta.msn.com/ encyclopedia_761574805/African_Art.html›.
	In-text	("African Arts" 13: 137) (Chanda)
Reference book, hard copy and online	Works Cited	Pendergast, Sara, and Tom Pendergast, eds. Reference Guide to World Literature. 3rd ed. 2 vols. Detroit: St. James Press/ Thomson-Gale, 2003. Cannon, John, ed. Oxford Companion to British History. New York: Oxford UP, 2002. ‹http://www.oxfordreference.com/

Reference book (*continued*)		views/BOOK_SEARCH.html?book=t110& subject=s11>. Cicioni, Mirna, "The periodic table (Il sistema periodico), prose by Primo Levi, 1975." Reference Guide to World Literature. Ed. Sara Pendergast and Tom Pendergast. 3rd ed. 2 vols. Detroit: St. James Press/Thomson-Gale, 2003. 2: 1447. "Polytheism." The New Dictionary of Cultural Literacy. Ed. E. D. Hirsch Jr., Joseph F. Kett, and James Trefil. 3rd ed. Boston: Houghton Mifflin, 2002. 2 Feb. 2004 <http://www .bartleby.com/59/5/polytheism.html>. ▶ This is a hard-copy book that is also available online. "Napoleon I." The Biographical Dictionary. 2004. S-9 Technologies. 5 Jan. 2004 <http:// www.s9.com/biography/search.html>
	In-text	(Pendergast and Pendergast) (Cannon) (Cicioni 2: 1447) ("Polytheism") ("Napoleon I")
Dictionary, hard copy, online, and CD-ROM	Works Cited	"Historiography." Merriam-Webster's Collegiate Dictionary. 11th ed. 2003. ▶ You can omit the publisher information. "Protest, v." Compact Edition of the Oxford English Dictionary. 1971 ed. 2: 2335. ▶ The word "protest" is both a noun and a verb, and I am citing the verb here. "Pluck, n." Def. 1. Oxford English Dictionary. Ed. J. A. Simpson and E. S. C. Weiner. 2nd ed. Oxford: Clarendon P, 1989. Oxford UP. 5 Jan. 2004 <http://dictionary.oed.com/cgi/ entry/00181836>. ▶ There are two separate entries for the noun *pluck*, and I am citing the first, hence n. Def. 1. The second is for an obscure fish.

"Balustrade." Microsoft Encarta Online
Dictionary. 2004. Microsoft. 5 Jan. 2004
<http://encarta.msn.com/dictionary_/
balustrade.html>.
"Citation." American Heritage Dictionary of the
English Language. 4th ed. CD-ROM. Boston:
Houghton Mifflin, 2000.

In-text
("Protest" 2: 2335)
(Compact OED 2: 2335)
("Citation") or (American Heritage Dictionary)

Bible | Works Cited

Tanakh: The Holy Scriptures: The New JPS
Translation according to the Traditional
Hebrew Text. Philadelphia: Jewish
Publication Society, 1985.

▸ The Bible does *not* usually appear in Works
Cited, although you can include it if you wish to
cite a particular version or translation.

In-text

Genesis 1.1, 1.3–5, 2.4.

▸ Books may be abbreviated, such as Gen. 1.1,
1.3–5, 2.4.

▸ Abbreviations for the next four books are Ex.,
Lev., Num., and Deut. Abbreviations for other
books are easily found with a Web search for
"abbreviations + Bible."

Speech,
academic
talk, or
course
lecture

Works Cited

Ferrell, Will. "Class Day Speech." Speech at
Harvard. Cambridge, MA. 4 June
2003.
Kamhi, Michelle. "Rescuing Art from 'Visual
Culture.'" Speech to annual convention of the
National Art Education Association.
Minneapolis, MN. 7 Apr. 2003.
Doniger, Wendy. Course lecture. U of Chicago.
Chicago, IL. 12 Mar. 2004.

▸ Or, using a more descriptive name for an
untitled lecture:
Doniger, Wendy. Course lecture on evil in Hindu
mythology. U of Chicago. Chicago, IL. 12 Mar.
2004.

Speech (*continued*)	In-text	(Ferrell)
		(Kamhi)
		(Doniger)

Interview, personal, telephone, or in print	Works Cited	King, Coretta Scott. Personal interview. 14 Jan. 2004.
		Wiesel, Elie. Telephone interview. 16 Feb. 2004.
		Arroyo, Gloria Macapagal. "A Time for Prayer." Interview with Michael Schuman. Time. 28 July 2003. 13 Jan. 2004 ⟨http://www.time.com/time/nation/article/0,8599,471205,00.html⟩.
	In-text	(King)

Personal communication	Works Cited	Wills, Gary. Conversation with author. 2 June 2005.
		Deis, Elizabeth. E-mail to author. 3 June 2005.
		▶ Unlike some other formats, MLA includes e-mails, conversations, and other personal communications in the Works Cited, even if they are not generally available to others.
		Vicinus, Martha. "Sweetland Conference; title for talk." E-mail to author. 22 Apr. 2005.
		Art Institute of Chicago. E-news. Apr. 2005 [e-mail sent to members]. 14 Apr. 2005.
		▶ If a personal communication is publicly archived, add the URL at the end of the citation.
	In-text	(Deis, e-mail)
		(Vicinus, e-mail) or (Vicinus, "Sweetland Conference")
		(Art Institute of Chicago, E-news)

| Poem | Works Cited | Bishop, Elizabeth. "The Fish." The Complete Poems, 1927–1979. New York: Noonday Press/Farrar, Straus and Giroux, 1983. 42–44. |

Lowell, Robert. "For the Union Dead." <u>The Top
500 Poems</u>. Ed. William Harmon. New York:
Columbia UP, 1992. 1061–63.

In-text | (Bishop 42–44) or (Bishop, "The Fish" 42–44) or
("The Fish" 42–44) or (42–44)

▸ For poems such as "The Fish," you can note the
verse and lines separated by periods or state
(lines 10–12).

(Lowell 1061–63) or (Lowell, "Union Dead"
1061–63)

| Play, text | Works Cited | Shakespeare, <u>Romeo and Juliet</u>. |

▸ If you wish to cite a specific edition, then:
Shakespeare, <u>Romeo and Juliet</u>. Ed. Brian
Gibbons. London: Methuen, 1980.

In-text | (Shakespeare, <u>Romeo and Juliet</u> 1.3.12–15) or
(<u>Romeo and Juliet</u> 1.3.12–15) or
(1.3.12–15) if the play's name is clear in the text.

▸ This refers to act 1, scene 3, lines 12–15
(separated by periods).

Performance | Works Cited | <u>Kiss</u>. Chor. Susan Marshall. Music Arvo Pärt.
of play or
dance

Perf. Cheryl Mann, Tobin Del Cuore. Hubbard
Street Dance Chicago. Joan W. and Irving B.
Harris Theater for Music and Dance, Chicago.
Mar. 12, 2004.

<u>Topdog/Underdog</u>. By Suzan Lori-Parks. Dir.
Amy Morton. Perf. K. Todd Freeman, David
Rainey. Steppenwolf Theater, Chicago. 2 Nov.
2003.

▸ If you are concentrating on one person's work
in theater, music, dance, or other collaborative
arts, put that person's name first. For example,
if you are focusing on David Rainey's acting:

Rainey, David, perf. <u>Topdog/Underdog</u>. By
Suzan Lori-Parks. Dir. Amy Morton . . .

▸ If, by contrast, you are focusing on Amy
Morton's directing or on directing in general:

Performance (*continued*)		Morton, Amy, dir. Topdog/Underdog. By Suzan Lori-Parks. Perf. David Rainey . . .
	In-text	(Kiss) (Topdog/Underdog) or (Rainey) or (Morton)
Television program	Works Cited	"Bart vs. Lisa vs. 3rd Grade." The Simpsons. Writ. T. Long. Dir. S. Moore. Episode: 1403 F55079. Fox. 17 Nov. 2002.
	In-text	("Bart vs. Lisa")
Film	Works Cited	Godfather II. Dir. Francis Ford Coppola. Perf. Al Pacino, Robert De Niro, Robert Duvall, Diane Keaton. Screenplay Francis Ford Coppola and Mario Puzo based on the novel by Mario Puzo. Paramount Pictures, 1974. DVD. Paramount Home Video, Godfather DVD Collection, 2003. ▸ Required: title, director, studio, and year released. Include them, or you will sleep with the fishes. ▸ Optional: actors, producers, screenwriters, editors, cinematographers, and other information. Include what you need for analysis in your paper, in order of their importance to your analysis. Their names appear between the title and the distributor. ▸ If you are concentrating on one person's work, put that person's name and role (such as performer) first, before the title: Coppola, Francis Ford, dir. Godfather II. Perf. Al Pacino, Robert De Niro, Robert Duvall, Diane Keaton. Paramount Pictures, 1974. DVD. Paramount Home Video, Godfather DVD Collection, 2003.
	In-text	(Godfather II)

Artwork, original	Works Cited	Tintoretto, Jacopo Robusti. The Birth of John the Baptist. 1550s. Oil on canvas, 181 x 266 cm. Hermitage, St. Petersburg. ▸ Year, size, and artistic medium are optional.
	In-text	(Tintoretto) or (Tintoretto, Birth of John the Baptist)
Artwork, reproduction	Works Cited	Tintoretto, Jacopo Robusti. The Birth of John the Baptist. 1550s. Hermitage, St. Petersburg. In Tintoretto: Tradition and Identity. By Tom Nichols. London: Reaktion Books, 1999. 47.
	In-text	(Tintoretto) or (Tintoretto, Birth of John the Baptist)
Artwork, online	Works Cited	Tintoretto, Jacopo Robusti. The Birth of John the Baptist. 1550s. Hermitage, St. Petersburg. State Hermitage Museum. 5 Jan. 2004 ‹http://www.hermitage.ru/html_En/index .html›. Tintoretto, Jacopo Robusti. The Birth of John the Baptist (detail). 1550s. Hermitage, St. Petersburg. CGFA-Virtual Art Museum. 5 Jan. 2004 ‹http://cgfa.floridaimaging.com/t/ p-tintore1.htm›. ▸ The same artwork accessed through the museum's site and another site. Note that the sponsors of the different Web sites are listed, as well as their URLs.
	In-text	(Tintoretto) or (Tintoretto, Birth of John the Baptist)
Photograph	Works Cited	Adams, Ansel. Monolith, the Face of Half Dome, Yosemite National Park. 1927. Art Institute, Chicago.
	In-text	(Adams) or (Adams, Monolith)

Figures: map, chart, graph, or table	Works Cited	"Electoral Vote Map." Map. Election 2000. 30 Aug. 2004 ‹http://www.usatoday.com/news/vote2000/electfront.htm›.

▶ MLA treats maps like anonymous books.

"Ethnic Population Transfers." Map. In Chaim D. Kaufmann, "When All Else Fails: Ethnic Population Transfers and Partitions in the Twentieth Century." International Security 23 (Fall 1998): 120–56.

▶ Or

Kaufmann, Chaim D. "When All Else Fails: Ethnic Population Transfers and Partitions in the Twentieth Century." International Security 23 (Fall 1998): 120–56.
("Electoral Vote Map")
("Ethnic Population Transfers") or (Kaufman, 137, map 2)

Musical recording	Works Cited	Johnson, Robert. "Come On in My Kitchen (Take 1)." Rec. 23 Nov. 1936. Robert Johnson: King of the Delta Blues Singers. Expanded edition. Columbia/Legacy, CK 65746, 1998.

Allman Brothers Band. "Come On in My Kitchen." By Robert Johnson. Shades of Two Worlds. Sony, 1991.
Barber, Samuel. "Cello Sonata, for cello and piano, Op. 6." Barber: Adagio for Strings, Violin Concerto, Orchestral and Chamber Works. Disc 2. St. Louis Symphony. Cond. Leonard Slatkin. Cello, Alan Stepansky. Piano, Israela Margalit. EMI Classics 74287, 2001.

▶ The catalog numbers are optional but helpful.
▶ There is no need to say that a recording is on CD. However, if it is on cassette, LP, or some other medium, that should be listed just before the publisher. For example:

Holloway, Stanley. "Get Me to the Church on Time." <u>My Fair Lady, Original London Cast Recording</u>. Book and lyrics, Alan Jay Lerner. Music, Frederick Loewe. Rec. 1958. Audiocassette. Broadway/Legacy 060539, 1998.

▸ If you are concentrating on one person's work, such as the pianist, her name can come first:

Margalit, Israela, piano. "Cello Sonata, for cello and piano, Op. 6." <u>Barber: Adagio for Strings, Violin Concerto, Orchestral and Chamber Works</u>. Disc 2. St. Louis Symphony. Cond. Leonard Slatkin. Cello, Alan Stepansky. EMI Classics 74287, 2001.

	In-text	(Johnson) or (Johnson, "Come On in My Kitchen") (Allman Brothers) or (Allman Brothers, "Come On in My Kitchen") (Holloway) or (Holloway, "Get Me to the Church on Time") (Margalit) or (Margalit, "Cello Sonata")
Sheet music	Works Cited	Bach, Johann Sebastian. <u>Toccata and Fugue in D Minor</u>. 1708. BWV 565. Arr. Ferruccio Benvenuto Busoni for solo piano. New York: G. Schirmer LB1629, 1942. ▸ This piece was written in 1708 and has the standard Bach classification BWV 565. The arrangement is published by G. Schirmer, with their catalog number LB1629.
	In-text	(<u>Toccata and Fugue in D Minor</u>) or (Bach, <u>Toccata and Fugue in D Minor</u>)
Liner notes	Works Cited	Reich, Steven. Liner notes. <u>Different Trains</u>. Kronos Quartet. Elektra/Nonesuch 9 79176-2, 1988.
	In-text	(Reich, <u>Different Trains</u>)

Government document, hard copy and online	Works Cited	Cong. Rec. 23 July 2003: 2468–72. United States. Cong. Senate. Committee on Armed Services. Hearings on S. 758, A Bill to Promote the National Security by Providing for a National Defense Establishment. 80th Cong., 1st sess., 1947. Freedman, Stephen. Four-Year Impacts of Ten Programs on Employment Stability and Earnings Growth. The National Evaluation of Welfare-to-Work Strategies. Washington, DC: U.S. Department of Education. 2000. ERIC Document Reproduction Service No. ED450262. United States. Department of State. China—25th Anniversary of Diplomatic Relations. Press Statement. 31 Dec. 2003. 5 Jan. 2004 ‹http://www.state.gov/r/pa/prs/ps/2003/27632.htm›.
	In-text	(Cong. Rec. 23 July 2003: 2468–72) (U.S. Cong., Senate, Committee on Armed Services) ▸ If you are only referencing one item from that committee, then in-text citations don't need to include the hearing number or report. (U.S. Cong., Senate, Committee on Armed Services, Hearings on S. 758, 1947) ▸ If you refer to several items from the committee, indicate which one you are citing. You can shorten that after the first use: (Hearings on S. 758) (Freedman) or (Freedman, Four-Year Impacts) (U.S. Department of State)
Software	Works Cited	Dreamweaver MX 2004. San Francisco: Macromedia, 2003.
	In-text	(Dreamweaver MX 2004)

Database	Works Cited	Internet Movie Database (IMDb). 2004. Internet Movie Database. 6 Jan. 2004 <http://www.imdb.com/>.
		Corpus Scriptorum Latinorum database of Latin literature. 2003. Forum Romanum. 5 Jan. 2004 <http://www.forumromanum.org/literature/index.html>.
		► For a specific item within this database:
		Caesar, Gaius Julius. Commentarii de bello civili. Ed. A. G. Peskett. Loeb Classical Library. London: W. Heinemann, 1914. Corpus Scriptorum Latinorum database of Latin literature. 2003. Forum Romanum. 5 Jan. 2004 <http://www.thelatinlibrary.com/caes.html>.
	In-text	(IMDb)
		(Corpus Scriptorum Latinorum)
		(Caesar) or (Caesar, Commentarii de bello civili)
Web site, entire	Works Cited	Digital History. Ed. Steven Mintz. 2003. U of Houston et al. 6 Jan. 2004. <http://www.digitalhistory.uh.edu/index.cfm?>.
		Internet Public Library (IPL). 2004. School of Information, U of Michigan. 7 Jan. 2004 <http://www.ipl.org/>.
	In-text	(Internet Public Library) or (IPL)
Web page, with author	Works Cited	Lipson, Charles. "Advice on Getting a Great Recommendation." Web page. 2003. 6 Jan. 2004 <http://www.charleslipson.com/courses/Getting-a-good-recommendation.htm>.
		► If the URL takes up more than one line, break *after* a single or double slash and *before* a period, a comma, a hyphen, an underline, or a number sign.

Web page, with author (*continued*)		▶ MLA currently suggests listing the date when you accessed a particular Web file. *The Chicago Manual of Style* now recommends against it, unless there is a reason.
	In-text	(Lipson) or (Lipson, "Advice")
		▶ Web pages and other online documents may not have pages. You may, however, be able to cite to a specific section (Lipson, sec. 7) or paragraph (Lipson, pars. 3–5).
Web page, no author	Works Cited	"I Love Lucy: Series Summary." Web page. Sitcoms Online. 2004. 28 Apr. 2005 ‹http://www.sitcomsonline.com/ilovelucy.html›.
	In-text	("I Love Lucy") or ("I Love Lucy: Series Summary")
Weblog, entry or comment	Works Cited	Jerz, Dennis. "How to Cite a Weblog and Weblog Comments in MLA Style." Weblog entry. 11 Dec. 2003. Kairosnews: A Weblog for Discussing Rhetoric, Technology, and Pedagogy. 2 Jan. 2004 ‹http://kairosnews.org/node/view/3542›.
		Kiwi (Janice Walker). "Citing Weblogs." Weblog comment. 3 Dec. 2003. Kairosnews: A Weblog for Discussing Rhetoric, Technology, and Pedagogy. 3 Jan. 2004 ‹http://kairosnews.org/node/view/3542›.
		Cowen, Tyler. "Trial by Jury." Weblog entry. 24 Dec. 2003 Volokh Conspiracy. 6 Jan. 2004 ‹http://volokh.com/›.
		Chafetz, Josh. Untitled Weblog entry. 27 Dec. 2003, 12:06 p.m. OxBlog. 29 Dec. 2003 ‹http://oxblog.blogspot.com/›.
		▶ Chafetz's posting had no title and is one of several he posted to this group blog on the same day. Listing the time identifies it.
	In-text	(Jerz) or (Jerz, "How to Cite a Weblog")

E-mail	Works Cited	Leis, Kathy. "Re: New Orleans family." E-mail to Karen Turkish. 3 Jan. 2006.
		Mattli, Walter. E-mail to the author. 7 Feb. 2006.
	In-text	(Leis)
		(Mattli)

Electronic newsgroups and forums	Works Cited	Schlapfer, Gary D. "Laptop Woes." Online posting. 21 Oct. 2005. EDTECH [Educational Technology]. 23 Oct. 2005 ‹http://groups .google.com/group/bit.listserv.edtech/ browse_thread/thread/a337a7e971a36e74/ d1b35631307859fa?hl=en #d1b35631307859fa›.
		Jbcarr. "Re: I'm thinking roses." Online posting. 20 Oct. 2005. Roses Forum. 24 Oct. 2005 ‹http://forums2.gardenweb.com/forums/ load/roses/msg1010162524239.html?4›.
	In-text	(Schlapfer)
		(Jbcarr)

MLA uses abbreviations frequently. Here are the most common:

MLA: COMMON ABBREVIATIONS IN WORKS CITED

and others	et al.	especially	esp.	paragraph	par.
appendix	app.	figure	fig.	part	pt.
book	bk.	note	n	pseudonym	pseud.
chapter	ch. or chap.	notes	nn	translator	trans.
compare	cf.	number	no.	verse	v.
document	doc.	opus	op.	verses	vv.
edition	ed.	page	p.	versus	vs.
editor	ed.	pages	pp.	volume	vol.

Note: All abbreviations are lowercase, usually followed by a period. Most form their plurals by adding "s." The exceptions are note (n → nn), opus (op. → opp.), page (p. → pp.), and translator (same abbreviation).

In citing poetry, do not use abbreviations for "line" or "lines" since a lowercase "l" is easily confused with the number one. Use either the full word or, if the meaning is clear, simply the number.

FAQS ABOUT MLA CITATIONS

How do I handle the citation when one author quotes another?
That happens frequently, as in Donald Kagan's book *The Peloponnesian War*, which often quotes Thucydides. Using MLA style, you might write:

> Kagan approvingly quotes Thucydides, who says that Athens acquired this vital site "because of the hatred they already felt toward the Spartans" (qtd. in Kagan 14).

In your Works Cited, you include Kagan but *not* Thucydides.

Some MLA citations, such as newspaper articles, use the names of months. Which ones should I abbreviate and which ones should I spell out?
Use three-letter abbreviations for all but the short names: May, June, and July.

5 APA CITATIONS FOR THE SOCIAL SCIENCES, EDUCATION, ENGINEERING, AND BUSINESS

APA citations are widely used in psychology, education, engineering, business, and the social sciences. Like MLA citations, they are in-text. They use notes only for analysis and commentary, not to cite references. Unlike MLA, however, APA emphasizes the year of publication, which comes immediately after the author's name. That's probably because as scholarship cumulates in the sciences and empirical social sciences (where APA is used), it is important to know whether the research was conducted recently and whether it came before or after other research. At least that's the rationale.

Detailed information on the APA system is available in

- *Publication Manual of the American Psychological Association*, 5th ed. (Washington, DC: American Psychological Association, 2001).

Like *The Chicago Manual of Style* and MLA style books, the APA manual should be available in your library's reference section. For more details on engineering papers, you can also consult an online guide from the American Society of Civil Engineers, available at http://www.pubs.asce.org/authors/index.html#manreq.

To get started, let's look at APA references for a journal article, a chapter in an edited book, and a book as they appear at the end of a paper. APA calls this a "Reference List." (MLA calls it "Works Cited," and Chicago calls it a "Bibliography.")

Lipson, C. (1991). Why are some international agreements informal? *International Organization, 45*, 495–538.

Lipson, C. (1994). Is the future of collective security like the past? In G. Downs (Ed.), *Collective security beyond the cold war* (pp. 105–131). Ann Arbor: University of Michigan Press.

Lipson, C. (2003). *Reliable partners: How democracies have made a separate peace.* Princeton, NJ: Princeton University Press.

This list for the distinguished author C. Lipson follows another APA rule. All entries for a single author are arranged by year of publication, beginning with the earliest. If there were two entries for a particular year, say 2004, they would be alphabetized by title and the first would be labeled (2004a), the second (2004b). Also note the APA's rules for capitalizing book and article titles. They are treated like sentences, with only the first words capitalized. If there's a colon in the title, the first word after the colon is also capitalized. Proper nouns are capitalized, of course, just as they are in sentences.

In these reference lists, single-author entries precede those with co-authors. So Pinker, S. (as a sole author) would proceed Pinker, S., & Jones, B. In the APA system, multiple authors are joined by an ampersand "&" rather than the word "and." It is not clear why. Just accept it as a rule, like how many minutes are in a soccer game.

The authors' first names are always reduced to initials. Pagination is not included for in-text references, except for direct quotes (where the pages are preceded by "p." or "pp."). That makes it different from the other systems, as does its frequent use of commas and parentheses.

When works are cited in the text, the citation includes the author's name, for example (Wilson, 2004d), unless the author's name has already been mentioned in that sentence. If the sentence includes the author's name, the citation omits it. For instance: Nye (2004) presents considerable data to back up his claims.

The examples in this section focus on the social sciences, education, engineering, and business, where APA citations are most widely used, just as the MLA examples focus on the humanities, where that style is common.

To make it easy to find the APA citations you need, I've listed them here alphabetically, along with the pages where they are described.

INDEX OF APA CITATIONS IN THIS CHAPTER

APA: REFERENCE LIST AND IN-TEXT CITATIONS

Book, one author	Reference list	Mandelbaum, M. (2002). *The ideas that conquered the world: Peace, democracy, and free markets in the twenty-first century.* New York: Public Affairs.
		Lundy, C. (2003). *Social work and social justice: A structural approach to practice.* Peterborough, ON: Broadview Press.
		▶ Canadian provinces are abbreviated with two letters.
	In-text	(Mandelbaum, 2002)
		(Lundy, 2003)
Books, several by same author	Reference list	Elster, J. (1989a). *The cement of society: A study of social order.* Cambridge: Cambridge University Press.
		Elster, J. (1989b). *Nuts and bolts for the social sciences.* Cambridge: Cambridge University Press.
		Elster, J. (1989c). *Solomonic judgements: Studies in the limitations of rationality.* Cambridge: Cambridge University Press; Paris: Editions de la Maison des sciences de l'homme.

Books, several by same author (*continued*)		Elster, J., & Moene, K. O. (Eds.). (1989). *Alternatives to capitalism*. Cambridge: Cambridge University Press. ▶ Note that the author's name is repeated. APA does not use dashes for repetition. ▶ When the same author or coauthors have several publications in the same year, list them alphabetically (by the first significant word in the title). Label them as "a," "b," and "c." The last item by Elster is *not* labeled "d" because its authorship is different. ▶ Coauthored books like Elster & Moene follow a writer's single-author ones, in the alphabetical order of the second author's name.
	In-text	(Elster, 1989a, 1989b, 1989c; Elster & Moene, 1989)
Book, multiple authors	Reference list	Reiter, D., & Stam, A. C. (2002). *Democracies at war*. Princeton, NJ: Princeton University Press. ▶ Name the first six authors, then add "et al."
	In-text	(Reiter & Stam, 2002) ▶ For two to five authors, name all authors in the first citation. Beginning with the second reference, name only the first author, then add "et al." ▶ For six or more authors, name only the first author, then add "et al." for all citations. ▶ Use "&" within parenthetical references but not in the text itself.
Book, multiple editions	Reference list	Strunk, W., Jr., & White, E. B. (2000). *The elements of style* (4th ed.). New York: Longman. ▶ If it says "revised edition" rather than 4th edition, use (Rev. ed.) in the same spot.
	In-text	(Strunk & White, 2000) ▶ To refer to a specific page for a quotation: (Strunk & White, 2000, p. 12)

Book, multiple editions, no author	Reference list	*National Partnership for Immunization reference guide* (2nd ed.). (2003). Alexandria, VA: National Partnership for Immunization. *Publication manual of the American Psychological Association* (5th ed.). (2001). Washington, DC: American Psychological Association. ▸ For multiple editions without authors, the form is *Title* (18th ed.). (year). City, STATE: Publisher.
	In-text	(National Partnership for Immunization [NPI], 2003) ▸ Subsequent references are (NPI, 2003) (American Psychological Association [APA], 2001) ▸ Subsequent references are (APA, 2001)
Book, edited	Reference list	Shweder, R. A., Minow, M., & Markus, H. (Eds.). (2002). *Engaging cultural differences: The multicultural challenge in liberal democracies*. New York: Russell Sage Foundation Press. Katznelson, I., & Shefter, M. (Eds.). (2002). *Shaped by war and trade: International influences on American political development*. Princeton, NJ: Princeton University Press.
	In-text	(Shweder, Minow, & Markus, 2002) (Katznelson & Shefter, 2002)
Book, online	Reference list	Reed, J. (1922). *Ten days that shook the world*. Project Gutenberg. Etext 3076. Retrieved January 12, 2004, from ftp://ibiblio.org/pub/docs/books/gutenberg/etext02/10daz10.txt ▸ APA does *not* put a period after the URL, making it different from most other reference styles.
	In-text	(Reed, 1922)
Multivolume work	Reference list	Pflanze, O. (1963–1990). *Bismarck and the development of Germany* (Vols. 1–3). Princeton, NJ: Princeton University Press.
	In-text	(Pflanze, 1963–1990)

| Single volume in a multivolume work | Reference list | Pflanze, O. (1990). *The period of fortification, 1880–1898: Vol. 3. Bismarck and the development of Germany.* Princeton, NJ: Princeton University Press. |
| | In-text | (Pflanze, 1990) |

| Reprint of earlier edition | Reference list | Smith, A. (1976). *An inquiry into the nature and causes of the wealth of nations.* E. Cannan (Ed.). Chicago: University of Chicago Press. (Original work published 1776) |
| | In-text | (Smith, 1776/1976) |

| Translated volume | Reference list | Weber, M. (1958). *The Protestant ethic and the spirit of capitalism.* T. Parsons (Trans.). New York: Charles Scribner's Sons. (Original work published 1904–1905) |
| | In-text | (Weber, 1904–1905/1958) |

| Chapter in edited book | Reference list | Keohane, R. (1983). The demand for international regimes. In S. Krasner (Ed.), *International regimes* (pp. 56–67). Ithaca, NY: Cornell University Press. |
| | In-text | (Keohane, 1983) |

| Journal article, one author | Reference list | Lipson, C. (1991). Why are some international agreements informal? *International organization, 45,* 495–538. |

- Notice that article titles are not in quotes.
- The journal's volume number is italicized, but the issue number and pages are not. The word "volume" (or "vol.") is omitted.
- There's no need to name a specific issue if the journal pages are numbered continuously throughout the year. However, if each issue begins with page 1, then the issue's number or month is necessary to find the article: *45*(2), 15–30.

| | In-text | (Lipson, 1991) |

Journal article, multiple authors	Reference list	Koremenos, B., Lipson, C., & Snidal, D. (2001). The rational design of international institutions. *International Organization, 55,* 761–799. Hansen, S. S., Munk-Jorgensen, P., Guldbaek, B., Solgard, T., Lauszus, K. S., Albrechtsen, N., et al. (2000). Psychoactive substance use diagnoses among psychiatric in-patients. *Acta Psychiatrica Scandinavica, 102,* 432–438. ▸ Name up to six authors, then add "et al."
	In-text	(Koremenos, Lipson, & Snidal, 2001) for first reference (Koremenos et al., 2001) for second reference and after
Journal article, online	Reference list	Conway, P. (2003). Truth and reconciliation: The road not taken in Namibia. *Online Journal of Peace and Conflict Resolution, 5*(1). Retrieved December 26, 2003, from http://www.trinstitute.org/ojpcr/5_1conway.htm Mitchell, T. (2002). McJihad: Islam in the U.S. global order. *Social Text, 20*(4), 1–18. Retrieved December 28, 2003, from JSTOR database: http://muse.jhu.edu/journals/xsocial_text/v020/20.4mitchell.html ▸ Your can omit the URL when citing well-known databases, such as JSTOR or PsycARTICLES.
	In-text	(Conway, 2003) (Mitchell, 2002)
Journal article, foreign language	Reference list	Maignan, I., & Swaen, V. (2004). La responsabilité sociale d'une organisation: Intégration des perspectives marketing et managériale. *Revue Française du Marketing, 200,* 51–66. ▸ Or Maignan, I., & Swaen, V. (2004). La responsabilité sociale d'une organisation: Intégration des perspectives marketing et managériale [The social responsibility of an organization: Integration of marketing and managerial perspectives]. *Revue Française du Marketing, 200,* 51–66.
	In-text	(Maignan & Swaen, 2004)

Newspaper or magazine article, no author	Reference list	The United States and the Americas: One history in two halves. (2003, December 13). *Economist*, 36. Strong aftershocks continue in California. (2003, December 26). *New York Times* [national ed.], p. A23. ▶ Newspaper page numbers include "p." or "pp."
	In-text	(United States and the Americas, 2003) (Strong aftershocks, 2003)
Newspaper or magazine article, with author	Reference list	Bruni, F. (2003, December 26). Pope pleads for end to terrorism and war. *New York Times* [national ed.], p. A21.
	In-text	(Bruni, 2003) or, if necessary, (Bruni, 2003, December 26)
Newspaper or magazine article, online	Reference list	Vick, K. (2003, December 27). Quake in Iran kills at least 5,000: Temblor devastates ancient city; officials appeal for assistance. *Washington Post* [online], p. A01. Retrieved January 2, 2004, from http://www .washingtonpost.com/wp-dyn/articles/ A31539-2003Dec26.html Jehl, D. (2004, January 1). U.S. hunts terror clues in case of 2 brothers. *New York Times* [online], p. A10. Retrieved February 6, 2004, from ProQuest Newspapers database.
	In-text	(Vick, 2003) or (Vick, 2003, December 27) (Jehl, 2004) or (Jehl, 2004, January 1)
Review	Reference list	Orr, H. A. (2003, August 14). What's not in your genes. [Review of the book *Nature via nurture: Genes, experience, and what makes us human*]. *New York Review of Books, 50,* 38–40.
	In-text	(Orr, 2003)

Unpublished paper, poster session, dissertation, or thesis	Reference list	Tsygankov, A. (2004, February). *Russia's Identity and foreign policy choices.* Paper presented at the Program on International Politics, Economics, and Security, University of Chicago. ► Only the month and year are needed for papers. Cheng, D. T., Smith, C. N., Thomas, T. L., Richards, J. A., Knight, D. C., Rao, S. M., et al. (2003, June). *Differential reinforcement of stimulus dimensions during human Pavlovian fear conditioning.* Poster session presented at the 9th Annual Meeting of the Organization for Human Brain Mapping, New York, NY. Reid, P. (1998). *Beginning therapists and difficult clients: An exploratory study.* Unpublished master's thesis, University of Massachusetts, Amherst. Gomez, C. (2003). *Identifying early indicators for autism in self-regulatory difficulties.* Unpublished doctoral dissertation. Auburn University, AL.
	In-text	(Tsygankov, 2004) (Cheng et al., 2003) (Reid, 1998) (Gomez, 2003)
Preprint	Reference list	Williams, A., Leen, T. K., Roberts, P. D. (2003). Random walks for spike-timing dependent plasticity. Preprint. arXiv: q-bio.NC/0312038. Retrieved December 26, 2003, from http://xxx.lanl.gov/PS_cache/q-bio/pdf/0312/0312038.pdf ► arXiv is a collection facility for scientific preprints. The "q-bio" number is its identification number there. ID numbers and URLs are valuable to readers who wish to follow your citation to the database itself.
	In-text	(Williams, Leen, & Roberts, 2003)

Abstract	Reference list	Kremer, M., & Zwane, A. P. (2005). Encouraging private sector research for tropical agriculture [Abstract]. *World Development, 33*, 87.

► Abstract obtained from original source. Use the same format to cite abstracts from published conference proceedings.

Albin, C. (2003). Negotiating international cooperation: Global public goods and fairness. *Review of International Studies, 29*, 365–85. Abstract obtained from *Peace Research Abstracts Journal, 42*, 2005, 6, Abstract No. 236625.

► Abstract obtained from secondary source.

	In-text	(Kremer & Zwane, 2005)

(Albin, 2003/2005)

► If the secondary abstract source is published in a different year than the primary source, cite both dates, separated by a slash.

Microfilm, microfiche	Reference list	U.S. House of Representatives. Records. Southern Claims Commission. (1871–1880). *First report (1871)*. Washington, DC: National Archives Microfilm Publication, P2257, Frames 0145–0165.

Conservative Party (UK). (1919). *Annual report of the executive committee to central council, March 11–November 18, 1919*. Archive of the British Conservative Party, Microfiche card 143. Woodbridge, CT: Gale/Primary Source Microfilm, 1998. (Original material located in Conservative Party Archive, Bodleian Library, Oxford, UK).

► You do not need to include the location of the original material, but you are welcome to.

	In-text	(U.S. House, 1871–1880)

(Conservative Party, 1919)

Encyclopedia, hard copy and online	Reference list	Balkans: History. (1987). In *Encyclopaedia Britannica* (15th ed., Vol. 14, pp. 570–588). Chicago: Encyclopaedia Britannica.

Balkans. (2003). *Encyclopaedia Britannica* [online].
Retrieved December 28, 2003, from http://
search.eb.com/eb/article?eu=119645
Graham, G. (2002). Behaviorism. In *Stanford
encyclopedia of philosophy* [online]. Retrieved
January 5, 2004, from http://plato.stanford.edu/
entries/behaviorism/

	In-text	(Balkans: History, 1987) (Balkans, 2003) (Graham, 2002)

Reference book, hard copy and online	Reference list	Pendergast, S., & Pendergast, T. (Eds.). (2003). *Reference guide to world literature* (3rd ed., 2 vols.). Detroit: St. James Press/ Thomson-Gale. Pendergast, S., & Pendergast, T. (Eds.). (2003). *Reference guide to world literature*. E-Book. (3rd ed.). Detroit: St. James Press. Colman, A. M. (2001). *A Dictionary of Psychology*. Oxford: Oxford University Press. Retrieved March 16, 2004, from http://www.oxfordreference.com/views/BOOK_SEARCH.html?book=t87 Woods, T. (2003). The social contract (du contract social), prose by Jean-Jacques Rousseau, 1762. In Pendergast, S., & Pendergast, T. (Eds.), *Reference guide to world literature* (3rd ed., Vol. 2, pp. 1512–1513). Detroit: St. James Press/ Thomson-Gale. Great Britain: Queen's speech opens Parliament. (2003, November 26). *FirstSearch*. Facts On File database. Accession no. 2003302680.
	In-text	(Pendergast & Pendergast, 2003) (Colman, 2001) (Woods, 2003) (Great Britain: Queen's speech, 2003)

Dictionary, hard copy, online, and CD-ROM	Reference list	Gerrymander. (2003). *Merriam-Webster's collegiate dictionary* (11th ed.). Springfield, MA: Merriam-Webster.

Dictionary (*continued*)		Protest, *v.* (1971). *Compact edition of the Oxford English dictionary* (Vol. 2, p. 2335). Oxford: Oxford University Press. ▶ The word "protest" is both a noun and a verb. Here, I am citing the verb. Class, *n.* (2003). *Dictionary.com.* Retrieved January 4, 2004, from http://dictionary.reference.com/ search?q=class Anxious. (2000). *American heritage dictionary of the English language* (4th ed.). CD-ROM. Boston: Houghton Mifflin.
	In-text	(Protest, 1971)
Speech, academic talk, or course lecture	Reference list	Szelenyi, I. (2003, August 17). Presidential address. American Sociological Association. Annual convention. Atlanta, GA. Woodward, A. (2004, April 14). Course lecture. University of Chicago. Chicago, IL.
	In-text	(Szelenyi, 2003) (Woodward, 2004)
Interview	Reference list	Arroyo, Gloria Macapagal. (2003). A Time for Prayer. Interview with Michael Schuman. *Time.* July 28, 2003. Retrieved Jan. 13, 2004, from http://www.time.com/time/nation/article/ 0,8599,471205,00.html
	In-text	(Arroyo, 2003) (E. O. Wilson, personal interview, February 1, 2004) ▶ The reference list includes printed interviews, like Arroyo's, but not personal communications such as private conversation, faxes, letters, or interviews since they cannot be accessed by other investigators. Therefore, in-text citations for personal communications (like the one for E. O. Wilson) should fully describe the item, including the full date.

Personal communication	Reference list	▶ Personal communications that cannot be retrieved or examined by third parties should not be included in the reference list. They should be fully described in the text.
	In-text	(David A. Grossberg, personal communication, May 6, 2005) ▶ This could be an e-mail, a conversation, a letter, a fax, a phone call, a memo, or a smoke signal.
Television program	Reference list	Long, T. (Writer), & Moore, S. D. (Director). (2002). Bart vs. Lisa vs. 3rd Grade [Television series episode]. In B. Oakley & J. Weinstein (Producers), *The Simpsons*. Episode: 1403 F55079. Fox.
	In-text	(*Simpsons*, 2002) or (Bart vs. Lisa, 2002)
Film	Reference list	Huston, J. (Director/Writer). (1941). *The Maltese falcon* [Motion picture]. Perf. Humphrey Bogart, Mary Astor, Peter Lorre, Sydney Greenstreet, Elisha Cook Jr. Based on novel by Dashiell Hammett. Warner Studios. U.S.: Warner Home Video, DVD (2000). ▶ Required: You must include the title, director, studio, and year released. ▶ Optional: the actors, producers, screenwriters, editors, cinematographers, and other information. Include what you need for analysis in your paper, in order of importance to your analysis. Their names appear between the title and the distributor.
	In-text	(*Maltese falcon*, 1941) or (*Maltese falcon*, 2000)
Photograph	Reference list	Adams, Ansel. (1927). *Monolith, the face of Half Dome, Yosemite National Park* [photograph]. Art Institute, Chicago.
	In-text	(Adams, 1927)

Figures: map, chart, graph, or table	Credit or explanation for figure or table	▸ Citation for a map, chart, graph, or table normally appears as a credit below the item rather than as an in-text citation. *Note:* Electoral vote map (2000), *Election 2000.* Retrieved August 30, 2004, from http://www.usatoday.com/news/vote2000/electfront.htm. *Note:* From Daryl G. Press (2001), The myth of air power in the Persian Gulf War and the future of warfare, *International Security* 26 (Fall): 17, fig. 2. ▸ Give a descriptive title to your maps, charts, graphs, and tables. With this description, the reader should understand the item without having to refer to the text. *Note:* All figures are rounded to nearest percentile. ▸ This is a general note explaining information in a table. *$p < .05$ **$p < .01$. Both are two-tailed tests. ▸ This is a probability note for a table of statistics.
	Reference list	Electoral vote map (2000). *Election 2000.* Retrieved August 30, 2004, from http://www.usatoday.com/news/vote2000/electfront.htm Press, Daryl G. (2001). The myth of air power in the Persian Gulf War and the future of warfare. *International Security* 26 (Fall): 5–44.
	In-text	(Electoral vote map [2000], 2004) (Press, 2001)
Government document, hard copy and online	Reference list	*A bill to promote the national security by providing for a national defense establishment: Hearings on S. 758 before the Committee on Armed Service, Senate.* 80th Cong., 1 (1947). ▸ "80th Cong., 1" refers to page one (not to the first session). If the reference was to testimony by a specific individual, that would appear after the date: (1947) (testimony of Gen. George Marshall). ▸ For documents printed by the Government Printing Office, give the full name rather than the initials GPO.

U.S. Census Bureau. (2006). *Statistical abstracts of the U.S.* Washington, DC: U.S. Census Bureau.

U.S. Department of Commerce. (2002). *A nation online: How Americans are expanding their use of the Internet.* Retrieved December 30, 2003, from http://www.ntia.doc.gov/ntiahome/dn/anationonline2.pdf

Federal Bureau of Investigation. (2001). *Investigation of Charles "Lucky" Luciano.* Part 1A. Retrieved January 2, 2004, from http://foia.fbi.gov/luciano/luciano1a.pdf

In-text   (*Bill to Promote National Security*, 1947)
(U.S. Census Bureau, 2006)
(U.S. Dept. of Commerce, 2002)
(FBI, 2001)

Software	Reference list	Dreamweaver MX 2004 [Computer software]. (2003). San Francisco: Macromedia. SPSS regression models (12.0 for Windows) [Computer software]. (2003). Chicago: SPSS.
	In-text	(Dreamweaver MX 2004, 2003) (SPSS Regression Models, 2003)
Database	Reference list	Bedford, VA, city of. (2004). *Property tax database.* Retrieved March 15, 2004, from http://www.ci.bedford.va.us/proptax/lookup.shtml *Intellectual Property Treaties, InterAm Database.* (2004). Tucson, AZ: National Law Center for Inter-American Free Trade. Retrieved March 15, 2004, from http://www.natlaw.com/database.htm
	In-text	(Bedford, 2004) (*Intellectual Property Treaties*, 2004)
Diagnostic test	Reference list	Tellegen, A., Ben-Porath, Y. S., McNulty, J. L., Arbisi, P. A., Graham, J. R., & Kaemmer, B. (2001). *MMPI-2 restructured clinical (RC) scales.* Minneapolis: University of Minnesota Press and Pearson Assessments.

Diagnostic test (*continued*)		Butcher, J. N., Graham, J. R., Ben-Porath, Y. S., Tellegen, A., Dahlstrom, W. G., & Kaemmer, B. (2001). *Minnesota multiphasic personality inventory-2 (MMPI-2): Manual for administration, scoring, and interpretation* (Rev. ed.). Minneapolis: University of Minnesota Press.
		▶ Manual for administering the test.
		Tellegen, A., Ben-Porath, Y. S., McNulty, J. L., Arbisi, P. A. & Graham, J. R. (2003). *The MMPI-2 restructured clinical (RC) scales: Development, validation, and interpretation.* Minneapolis: University of Minnesota Press and Pearson Assessments.
		▶ Interpretive manual for the test.
		Microtest Q assessment system software for MMPI-2. (2003). Version 5.07. Minneapolis: Pearson Assessments.
		▶ Scoring software for the test.
	In-text	(*MMPI-2 RC Scales*, 2001) (*MMPI-2 RC Scales*, 2003) (*Microtest Q*, 2003)
Diagnostic manual	Reference list	American Psychiatric Association. (2000). *Diagnostic and statistical manual of mental disorders* (4th ed. text revision [*DSM-IV-TR*]). Washington, DC: American Psychiatric Association Press.
	In-text	(American Psychiatric Association, *Diagnostic and statistical manual of mental disorders*, 2000) for the first use only (*DSM-IV-TR*) for second use and later. Title is italicized.
Web site, entire	Reference list	*Digital History* Web site. (2004). S. Mintz (Ed.). Retrieved January 10, 2004, from http://www .digitalhistory.uh.edu/index.cfm? *Internet Public Library* (IPL) (2003, November 17). Retrieved January 5, 2004, from http://www .ipl.org/

Yale University, History Department home page.
(2003). Retrieved January 6, 2004, from http://
www.yale.edu/history/

> If a Web site or Web page does not show a date
> when it was copyrighted or updated, then list
> (n.d.) where the year normally appears.

	In-text	(Digital History, 2004) (Internet Public Library, 2003) or (IPL, 2003) (Yale History Department home page, 2003)
Web page, with author	Reference list	Lipson, C. (2004). *Advice on getting a great recommendation.* Retrieved February 1, 2004, from http://www.charleslipson.com/courses/ Getting-a-good-recommendation.htm
	In-text	(Lipson, 2004)
Web page, no author	Reference list	*I Love Lucy*: Series summary. (2004). *Sitcoms Online.* Retrieved May 4, 2005, from http://www.sitcomsonline.com/ilovelucy.html
	In-text	(*I Love Lucy*: Series summary, 2004)
Weblog, entry or comment	Reference list	Drezner, D. (2004, February 1). Entry post. Retrieved February 2, 2004, from http://www .danieldrezner.com/blog/
	In-text	(Drezner, 2004)
E-mail or electronic newsgroup	Reference list	> Personal e-mails and non-archived discussion groups are not included in the reference list because they cannot be retrieved by third parties. You should include newsgroups, Listservs, and archived discussions if they can be accessed. Chicago Council on Foreign Relations. (2005, April 27). Blending Islam and democracy: Southeast Asia's unique experience [Msg]. *e-Chronicle*, May 2005. Posted to Chicago Council on Foreign Relations electronic mailing list, archived at http://www.ccfr.org/publications/ pdf/may05.pdf

| E-mail | In-text | (Andrew J. Aronson, MD, personal communication, May 4, 2005). |
| (*continued*) | | |

> ▸ The Aronson citation could be an e-mail, a letter, a fax, or a phone call. The in-text citation should give a full description because as a personal communication, it will not be included in the reference list.

(Chicago Council on Foreign Relations, 2005)

APA does not permit very many abbreviations in its reference lists. When it does, it sometimes wants them capitalized and sometimes not. Who knows why?

APA: COMMON ABBREVIATIONS IN REFERENCE LISTS

chapter	chap.	pages	pp.	supplement	Suppl.
edition	ed.	part	Pt.	translated by	Trans.
editor	Ed.	revised edition	Rev. ed.	volume	Vol.
number	No.	second edition	2nd ed.	volumes	Vols.
page	p.				

6 AAA CITATIONS
FOR ANTHROPOLOGY
AND ETHNOGRAPHY

The American Anthropological Association (AAA) has designed its own citation style for the discipline. Within the text, citations use a standard author-date format, such as (Fogelson 2004) or (Comaroff and Comaroff 2005). That's the same as the familiar APA system. The difference comes at the end of the paper, in References Cited. Here, the anthropology system places the author's name on a separate line and lists all the publications below it, in a special indented form. (It's a hanging indent so the date of publication stands out.) For example:

Gal, Susan
    2003 Movements of Feminism: The Circulation of Discourses about Women. *In* Recognition Struggles and Social Movements: Contested Identities, Power and Agency. Barbara Hobson, ed. Pp. 93–120. Cambridge: Cambridge University Press.

Sahlins, Marshall
    2000a Ethnographic Experience and Sentimental Pessimism: Why Culture Is Not a Disappearing Object. *In* Biographies of Scientific Objects. Lorraine Daston, ed. Pp. 158–293. Chicago: University of Chicago Press.
    2000b Waiting for Foucault. 3rd edition. Chicago: Prickly Paradigm Press.
    2004 Apologies to Thucydides: Understanding History as Culture and Vice Versa. Chicago: University of Chicago Press.

List the earliest works first. If an author has published more than one work in the same year, as Sahlins has for 2000, list them in alphabetical order and mark them "a," "b," and "c." If Sahlins has a coauthor, list that pairing on a separate line (as if they were a new author), below Sahlins as a single author.

Within the text, keep citations as simple as possible. That may be the author's name and the year of publication, such as (Silverstein 2006). If the sentence already includes the author's name, the citation can be even simpler:

Kelly (2005) offers a sophisticated argument on this point.

It is easy to include specific pages if you want to reference them. For example:

Kelly (2005:9–13) offers a sophisticated argument on this point.

You'll often want to include pages like this, and you'll need to when you quote an author.

The table below shows how to use AAA citations across a wide range of items. If you want more information, you can find it online at

- http://www.aaanet.org/pubs/style_guide.pdf

You can also find examples of citations using AAA style in the association's official journal, *American Anthropologist*.

Although AAA citations are always made with author-date references (in parentheses), your text may also include some explanatory notes. These footnotes or endnotes can be used to discuss supplementary issues; they cannot be used for citations. If you need to cite something within the note itself, simply use author-date references in parentheses, as you would elsewhere.

INDEX OF AAA CITATIONS IN THIS CHAPTER

AAA: REFERENCES CITED AND IN-TEXT CITATIONS

Book, one author	References Cited	Blackburn, Carole 2000 Harvest of Souls: The Jesuit Missions and Colonialism in North America, 1632–1650. Montreal: McGill-Queen's. Klima, Alan 2003 The Funeral Casino: Meditation, Massacre, and Exchange with the Dead in Thailand. Princeton, NJ: Princeton University Press. ▸ Book titles are not italicized.
	In-text	(Blackburn 2000) (Klima 2003) or, for specific pages or chapters: (Klima 2003:41) (Klima 2003:ch.4)
Books, several by same author	References Cited	Doniger, Wendy 1998 The Implied Spider: Politics and Theology in Myth. New York: Columbia University Press. 1999 Splitting the Difference: Gender and Myth in Ancient Greece and India. Chicago: University of Chicago Press. 2000 The Bedtrick: Tales of Sex and Masquerade. Chicago: University of Chicago Press. 2005 The Woman Who Pretended to Be Who She Was: Myths of Self-Imitation. New York: Oxford University Press. Doniger, Wendy, and Gregory Spinner 1998 Misconceptions: Female Imaginations and Male Fantasies in Parental Imprinting. Daedalus 127(1): 97–130.

Books,
several by
same author
(*continued*)

▸ Publications from the earliest year are listed first. When the same author or coauthors have several publications in the same year, list them alphabetically (by the first significant word in the title). Label them as "a," "b," and "c."

▸ Coauthored works follow a writer's single-author ones, in the alphabetical order of the second author's surname.

▸ Works are listed under an author's name only if they all have exactly the same author (or authors). Thus, the publications listed under Doniger do not include others written jointly with Gregory Spinner.

In-text

(Doniger 1998, 1999, 2000, 2005)
(Doniger and Spinner 1998)

Book,
multiple
authors

References
Cited

Mascia-Lees, Frances E., and Patricia Sharpe
2000 Taking a Stand in a Postfeminist World: Toward an Engaged Cultural Criticism. Albany: State University of New York Press.

▸ AAA does not indicate how many authors should be included. The APA, which has a similar format, names the first six authors and then adds "et al."

In-text

(Mascia-Lees and Sharpe 2000)

▸ Name up to two authors. For three or more, name only the first one and then use "et al."; for example:

(Mascia-Lees et al.)

Book,
multiple
editions

References
Cited

Hockings, Paul, ed.
2004 Principles of Visual Anthropology. 3rd edition. Berlin: Mouton de Gruyter.
Peacock, James L.
2001 The Anthropological Lens. Rev. edition. Cambridge: Cambridge University Press.

▸ To differentiate the English and American university towns:

Cambridge: Cambridge University Press.
Cambridge, MA: Harvard University Press.

	In-text	(Hockings 2004) (Peacock 2001) ► To refer to a specific page for a quotation: (Peacock 2001:12)

Book,
multiple
editions,
corporate
author
	References
	Cited
		American Psychological Association
		    2001 Publication Manual of the American
		        Psychological Association. 5th edition.
		        Washington, DC: American Psychological
		        Association.

	In-text	(American Psychological Association [APA] 2001) ► Subsequent references are (APA 2001).

Book,
anonymous
or no author
	References
	Cited
		Anonymous
		    2003 Golden Verses of the Pythagoreans.
		        Whitefish, MT: Kessinger.

	In-text	(Anonymous 2003)

Book,
edited
	References
	Cited
		Bond, George Clement, and Diane M. Ciekawy,
		    eds.
		    2001 Witchcraft Dialogues: Anthropological
		        and Philosophical Exchanges. Athens:
		        Ohio University Press.
		Vertovec, Steven, and Robin Cohen, eds.
		    2002 Conceiving Cosmopolitanism: Theory,
		        Context and Practice. Oxford: Oxford
		        University Press.

	In-text	(Bond and Ciekawy 2001) (Vertovec and Cohen 2002)

Book, online	References
	Cited
		Kumar, Nita
		    1992 Friends, Brothers, and Informants:
		        Fieldwork Memoirs of Banaras. Berkeley:
		        University of California Press. Electronic

Book, online (*continued*)		document, http://ark.cdlib.org/ark:/13030/ ft6xonb4g3/, accessed December 1, 2004.
	In-text	(Kumar 1992)
Multivolume work	References Cited	Stocking, George W., Jr., ed. 1983–1996 History of Anthropology. 8 vols. Madison: University of Wisconsin Press.
	In-text	(Stocking 1983–96)
Single volume in a multi-volume work	References Cited	Peregrine, Peter N., and Melvin Ember, eds. 2001 Encyclopedia of Prehistory, vol. 6: North America. New York: Kluwer Academic/ Plenum Publishers. Stocking, George W., Jr. 1991 History of Anthropology, vol. 7: Colonial Situations: Essays on the Contextualization of Ethnographic Knowledge. George W. Stocking Jr., ed. Madison: University of Wisconsin Press.
	In-text	(Peregrine and Ember 2001) (Stocking 1991)
Book in a series	References Cited	Whittaker, Andrea 2004 Abortion, Sin and the State in Thailand. ASAA Women in Asia Series. New York: Routledge.
	In-text	(Whittaker 2004)
Reprint of earlier edition	References Cited	Boas, Franz 2004[1932] Anthropology and Modern Life. New Brunswick, NJ: Transaction Publishers.
	In-text	(Boas 2004) or for a specific page (Boas 2004:43) ▶ In-text citations use only the reprint date.

| Translated volume | References Cited | Foucault, Michel
1977 Discipline and Punish: The Birth of Prison. Alan Sheridan, trans. New York: Pantheon Books. |
| | In-text | (Foucault 1977) |

| Chapter in edited book | References Cited | Silverstein, Michael
2000 Whorfianism and the Linguistic Imagination of Nationality. *In* Regimes of Language: Ideologies, Polities, and Identities. Paul V. Kroskrity, ed. Pp. 85–138. Santa Fe, NM: School of American Research Press.
▸ Chapter titles are not placed in quotes or italicized.

Doniger, Wendy
1995 Foreword. *In* Myth and Meaning. Claude Lévi-Strauss. Pp. vii–xv. New York: Schocken.
▸ Forewords, introductions, and afterwords are treated the same way, with pagination immediately before the place of publication. |
| | In-text | (Silverstein 2000)
(Doniger 1995) |

| Journal article, one author | References Cited | Bender, Barbara
2002 Time and Landscape. Current Anthropology 43:103–12.
▸ Article titles are not placed in quotes; journal titles are not italicized.
▸ There's no need to name a specific issue if the journal pages are numbered continuously throughout the volume. However, if each issue begins with page 1, then the issue's number or month is necessary to find the article: 43(2):15–30.

Jordt, Ingrid
2003 From Relations of Power to Relations of Authority: Epistemic Claims, Practices and Ideology in the Production of Burma's Political Order. Theme issue, "Knowledge and Verification," Social Analysis 47(1):65–76. |

| | In-text | (Bender 2002) |
| | | (Jordt 2003) |

| Journal article, multiple authors | References Cited | Knight, Vernon James, Jr., James A. Brown, and George E. Lankford
2001 On the Subject Matter of Southeastern Ceremonial Complex Art. Southeastern Archaeology 20:129–41.
▶ Name up to six authors in the References Cited, then add "et al." |
| | In-text | (Knight et al. 2001) for more than two authors |

Journal article, online	References Cited	Conway, Paul 2003 Truth and Reconciliation: The Road Not Taken in Namibia. Online Journal of Peace and Conflict Resolution, 5(1). Electronic document, http://www.trinstitute.org/ojpcr/5_1conway.htm, accessed December 1, 2004. Mitchell, Timothy 2002 McJihad: Islam in the U.S. Global Order. Social Text, 20(4):1–18. Electronic document, retrieved from JSTOR database: http://muse.jhu.edu/journals/social_text/v020/20.4mitchell.html, accessed December 1, 2004. ▶ You can omit the URL when citing well-known databases, such as JSTOR or PsycARTICLES. For example: Mitchell, Timothy 2002 McJihad: Islam in the U.S. Global Order. Social Text, 20(4):1–18. Electronic document, retrieved from JSTOR database, accessed December 1, 2004.
	In-text	(Conway 2003)
		(Mitchell 2002)

Newspaper or magazine article, no author	References Cited	Economist
		   2003 The United States and the Americas: One History in Two Halves. Economist, December 13: 36.
		New York Times
		   2003 Strong Aftershocks Continue in California. New York Times, December 26: A23 (national edition).

	In-text	(Economist 2003) or for multiple citations to 2003: (Economist 2003a) (New York Times 2003) or if necessary: (New York Times 2003a)
Newspaper or magazine article, with author	References Cited	Bruni, Frank 2003 Pope Pleads for End to Terrorism and War. New York Times, December 26: A21.
	In-text	(Bruni 2003) or for multiple citations to 2003: (Bruni 2003a)

Newspaper or magazine article, online	References Cited	Jehl, Douglas
		   2004 U.S. Hunts Terror Clues in Case of 2 Brothers. New York Times, January 1. Electronic document, ProQuest Newspapers database, accessed February 6, 2004.
		
		Vick, Karl
		   2003 Quake in Iran Kills at Least 5,000: Temblor Devastates Ancient City; Officials Appeal for Assistance. Washington Post, December 26. Electronic document, http://www.washingtonpost.com/wp-dyn/articles/A31539-2003Dec26.html, accessed January 2, 2004.

	In-text	(Jehl 2004) or (Jehl 2004a) (Jehl 2004b) (Vick 2003) or (Vick, December 26, 2003)

Review	References Cited	Orr, H. Allen 2003 *Review of* Nature via Nurture: Genes, Experience, and What Makes Us Human. New York Review of Books 50(August 14):38–40. Pye, Lucian W. 2004 *Review of* Fragments of Grace: My Search for Meaning in the Strife of South Asia. *In* Foreign Affairs (September/October). Electronic document, http://www.foreignaffairs.org/20040901fabook83560/pamela-constable/fragments-of-grace-my-search-for-meaning-in-the-strife-of-south-asia.html, accessed December 2, 2004.
	In-text	(Orr 2003) (Pye 2004)
Exhibition catalog	References Cited	Fitzhugh, William W., and Aron Crowell 1988 Crossroads of Continents: Cultures of Siberia and Alaska. Exhibition catalog. Washington, DC: Smithsonian Institution Press.
	In-text	(Fitzhugh and Crowell 1988)
Unpublished paper, thesis, or dissertation	References Cited	Russel y Rodríguez, Mónica 2002 Chicanas in Higher Ed; or, Making a Career from Scratch. Paper presented at the National Association for Chicana and Chicano Studies Annual Conference, Tucson, AZ, March 21. Magazine, Roger 2000 Stateless Contexts: Street Children and Soccer Fans in Mexico City. Ph.D. dissertation, Department of Anthropology, Johns Hopkins University. Brenneis, Donald N.d. Reforming Promise. Unpublished MS, Department of Anthropology, University of California, Santa Cruz.

▶ "MS" is in caps without a period.

Marlowe, Frank W.
  In press Mate Preferences among Hadza
    Hunter-Gatherers. *In* Human Nature.
▶ This refers to a work accepted for publication.

	In-text	(Russel y Rodríguez 2002)
		(Magazine 2000)
		(Brenneis n.d.)
		(Marlowe in press)

Microfilm, microfiche	References Cited	U.S. House of Representatives

U.S. House of Representatives
  1871 First Report. Southern Claims
    Commission. Records (1871–1880).
    Microfilm Publication P2257, Frames
    0145-0165. Washington, DC: National
    Archives.
Conservative Party (UK) Archive
  1919 Annual Report of the Executive Committee
    to Central Council. March 11–November 18.
    Microfiche card 143. Woodbridge, CT:
    Gale/Primary Source Microfilm, 1998.
    (Original material located in Conservative
    Party Archive, Bodleian Library, Oxford,
    UK.)
▶ You do not need to include the location of the
  original material, but you are welcome to.

	In-text	(U.S. House 1871)
		(Conservative Party 1919)

Archival materials and manuscript collections, hard copies and online — References Cited

Rice Ballard Papers
  N.d. Southern Historical Collection. Wilson
    Library, University of North Carolina,
    Chapel Hill.

▶ Or

Franklin, Isaac
  1831 Letter to R. C. Ballard, February 28. *In* Rice
    Ballard Papers, Southern Historical
    Collection. Wilson Library, University of
    North Carolina, Chapel Hill.

Archival
materials
(*continued*)

▸ In the text or explanatory notes, you may cite directly to Isaac Franklin's letter to R. C. Ballard and include it in your References Cited. Or you may refer to the letter in the text and cite to the collection (Rice Ballard Papers).

Boston YWCA Papers
  N.d. Schlesinger Library, Radcliffe Institute for Advanced Study, Harvard University.

▸ Or

Lamson, Mary Swift
  1891 An Account of the Beginning of the B.Y.W.C.A. MS [n.d.] and accompanying letter. Boston YWCA Papers. Schlesinger Library, Radcliffe Institute for Advanced Study, Harvard University.

▸ If Lamson's account is the only item cited from these papers, then it would be listed in the References Cited.

Taft, Horatio Nelson
  1861–62 Diary. Vol. 1, January 1, 1861–April 11, 1862. Manuscript Division, Library of Congress. Electronic document, http://memory.loc.gov/ammem/tafthtml/tafthome.html, accessed May 30, 2004.

In-text:

(Rice Ballard Papers n.d.)
(Boston YWCA Papers n.d.)
(Lamson 1891)
(Taft 1861–62)

Encyclopedia, hard copy and online

References Cited

Encyclopaedia Britannica
  1987 Balkans: History. 15th edition. Vol. 14. Pp. 570–88. Chicago: Encyclopaedia Britannica.
  2004 Balkans. Electronic document, http://search.eb.com/eb/article?eu=119645, accessed January 4, 2004.
Brumfiel, Elizabeth M.
  2001 States and Civilizations, Archaeology of. *In* International Encyclopedia of Social and Behavioral Sciences. N. J. Smelser

and P. B. Baltes, eds. Pp. 14983–88. Oxford:
Elsevier Science.

Graham, George

2002 Behaviorism. *In* Stanford Encyclopedia of
Philosophy. Electronic document, http://
plato.stanford.edu/entries/behaviorism/,
accessed November 30, 2004.

Haas, Jonathan

2001 Kayenta Anasazi. *In* Encyclopedia of
Prehistory: North America, vol. 6. Peter N.
Peregrine and Melvin Ember, eds. Pp. 40–42.
New York: Kluwer Academic/Plenum Publishers.

In-text

(Encyclopaedia Britannica 1987)

(Encyclopaedia Britannica 2004)

(Brumfiel 2001)

(Graham 2002)

(Haas 2001)

Reference book, hard copy and online	References Cited	Pendergast, Sara, and Tom Pendergast, eds. 2003 Reference Guide to World Literature. 2 vols. 3rd edition. Detroit: St. James Press/Thomson-Gale. Pendergast, Sara, and Tom Pendergast, eds. 2003 Reference Guide to World Literature. eBook. 3rd edition. Detroit: St. James Press/Thomson-Gale. Colman, Andrew M. 2001 A Dictionary of Psychology. Oxford: Oxford University Press. Electronic document, http://www.oxfordreference.com/views/BOOK_SEARCH.html?book=t87, accessed March 16, 2004. Great Britain: Queen's Speech Opens Parliament 2003 FirstSearch. Facts On File database. Accession no. 2003302680. November 26.
	In-text	(Pendergast and Pendergast 2003) ▶ For a specific page in a specific volume: (Pendergast and Pendergast 2003, vol. 2:619) (Colman 2001) (Great Britain: Queen's Speech 2003)

Dictionary, hard copy, online, and CD-ROM	References Cited	Merriam-Webster's Collegiate Dictionary
		  2003 Caste. 11th edition. Springfield, MA: Merriam-Webster.
		Compact Edition of the Oxford English Dictionary
		  1971 Protest, v. Oxford: Oxford University Press. Vol. 2:2335.
		  ▶ The word "protest" is both a noun and a verb. Here, I am citing the verb.
		
		Dictionary.com
		  2003 Class, n. Electronic document, http://dictionary.reference.com/search?q=class, accessed January 4, 2005.
		American Heritage Dictionary of the English Language
		  2000 Folklore. 4th edition. CD-ROM. Boston: Houghton Mifflin.
		Speake, Jennifer, ed.
		  2003 "Where MacGregor sits is the head of the table." *In* Oxford Dictionary of Proverbs. 4th edition. P. 161. Oxford: Oxford University Press.
		Winthrop, Robert H.
		  1991 Caste. *In* Dictionary of Concepts in Cultural Anthropology. Pp. 27–30. New York: Greenwood.

	In-text	(Merriam-Webster's Collegiate Dictionary 2003) (Compact Edition of the Oxford English Dictionary 1971) (Dictionary.com 2003) (American Heritage Dictionary 2000) (Speake 2003) (Winthrop 1991)

Speech, academic talk, or course lecture	References Cited	Lamphere, Louise
		  2001 Unofficial Histories: A Vision of Anthropology from the Margins. 2001 American Anthropological Association Presidential Address. Chicago, IL. December 1.
		Comaroff, John L.
		  2004 Course lecture. University of Chicago, Chicago, April 12.

| | In-text | (Lamphere 2001) |
| | | (Comaroff 2004) |

Interview	References Cited	Wilson, E. O.
		2004 Personal interview regarding biodiversity. Cambridge, MA, February 1.
		Douglas, Mary
		2003 Interview with John Clay. Electronic document, http://www.bhag.net/2001/2001douglasm/pdouglasm1.html, accessed November 30, 2004.
		▸ Unpublished personal communications are often identified parenthetically in the text, such as (John Doe, interview with author, May 1, 2005). Some authors include communications like this in References Cited; some don't. AAA seems to be of two minds. Their online style guide says to omit them, but articles in their official journals frequently include them. My suggestion: it's your choice, but be consistent and definitely include communications that can be accessed by your readers, such as items posted online.
	In-text	(Wilson 2004)
		(Douglas 2003)

Television program	References Cited	Moore, Steven Dean, dir.
		2002 Bart vs. Lisa vs. 3rd Grade. The Simpsons. Fox, November 17.
		▸ To emphasize the title, writer, or particular actor, put that name on the top line (and include the director in the line below):
		Long, Tim, writer
		2002 Bart vs. Lisa vs. 3rd Grade. Steven Dean Moore, dir. The Simpsons. Fox, November 17.
	In-text	(Moore 2002)
		(Long 2002)

Film	References Cited	Jackson, Peter, dir. 2003 The Lord of the Rings: The Return of the King. 201 min. New Line Cinema. Hollywood. Asch, Timothy, and Napoleon Chagnon, creators 1975 The Ax Fight. 30 min. Black-and-white. National Anthropological Archives and Human Studies Film Archives, SA-81.5.1. ▸ Or to emphasize the title rather than the creators: Ax Fight, The 1975 Timothy Asch and Napoleon Chagnon, creators. 30 min. Black-and-white. National Anthropological Archives and Human Studies Film Archives, SA-81.5.1. ▸ Films may be included in the References Cited or may be listed separately in a section entitled "Filmography References" or "Films Cited."
	In-text	(Jackson 2003) (Asch and Chagnon 1975) or (Ax Fight 1975)
Photograph	References Cited	Adams, Ansel 1927 Monolith, the Face of Half Dome, Yosemite National Park. Photograph. Chicago: Art Institute. ▸ Photographs are seldom included in reference lists. They are usually identified in the article itself, immediately beneath the photo. For example, a photo of rural houses might include this explanation: Typical sharecropper homes, Quitman County, Mississippi (April 2006) (Photo by Maude Schuyler Clay)
	In-text	(Adams 1927)
Figures: map, chart, graph, or table	Credit or explanation for figure or table	▸ Give a descriptive title to your maps, charts, photos, graphs, and tables. Place an identifying credit or clarifying information below the item, such as Dancing at Carnival, Rio de Janeiro (2005) (Photo by Eric Cartman)

President James Knox Polk, three-quarter-length portrait (1849) (Daguerreotype by Mathew Brady) (Collection of the Library of Congress)

Ceremonial grave markers (Mohawk) (Collection of Art Institute of Chicago)

All figures in this table are rounded to nearest percentile.

Two-tailed significance tests: $*p < .05$ $**p < .01$

▶ You may also need to list sources for a figure, map, chart, graph, or table. Here, for example, is a title for a table, with an asterisk after the title to identify the sources of information on which it is based. These sources (Jones and Smith) are identified by in-text citations on a line below the table. Full information about them appears in the References Cited.

Table 4: Fertility rates of Bedouins in Israel*
*Sources: Jones (2004), Smith (2005)

Musical recording	References Cited	Johnson, Robert 　1961　Cross Road Blues. *In* Robert Johnson: King of the Delta Blues Singers. New York: Columbia Records.
	In-text	(Johnson 1961)
Government document, hard copy and online	References Cited	U.S. Senate, Committee on Armed Services 　1947　Hearings on S. 758: A bill to promote the national security by providing for a national defense establishment. 80th Cong., 1st sess. U.S. Bureau of the Census 　2000　Statistical Abstracts of the U.S. Washington, DC: U.S. Bureau of the Census. U.S. Department of Commerce 　2002　A Nation Online: How Americans Are Expanding Their Use of the Internet. Electronic document, http://www.ntia.doc.gov/ntiahome/dn/anationonline2.pdf, accessed January 2, 2005.

Government document (*continued*)		UN Development Programme 2004 Human Development Report 2004: Cultural Liberty in Today's Diverse World. Electronic document, http://hdr.undp.org/reports/ global/2004/, accessed January 2, 2005.
	In-text	(U.S. Senate, Committee on Armed Service 1947) (U.S. Bureau of the Census 2000) (U.S. Dept. of Commerce 2002) (UN Development Programme 2004)
Database	References Cited	Anthropology Review Database N.d. ARD: Anthropology Review Database. http://wings.buffalo.edu/anthropology/ ARD/, accessed November 30, 2004. InterAm Database 2004 Intellectual Property Treaties. Tucson, AZ: National Law Center for Inter-American Free Trade. Electronic document, http://www .natlaw.com/database.htm, accessed November 30, 2004.
	In-text	(Anthropology Review Database n.d.) (InterAm Database 2004)
Website, entire	References Cites	Digital History Website N.d. Website. Sidney Mintz, ed. http://www .digitalhistory.uh.edu/index.cfm?, accessed February 10, 2004. ▸ AAA format spells "Website" as one word. Internet Public Library (IPL) 2004 Website, http://www.ipl.org/, accessed November 30, 2004. Harvard University, Department of Anthropology 2004 Website, http://www.fas.harvard.edu/ ∼anthro/, accessed November 30, 2004. ▸ If a Website or Web page does not show a date when it was copyrighted or updated, then list "N.d." where the year normally appears.

	In-text	(Digital History n.d.) (Internet Public Library 2004) or (IPL 2004) (Harvard University, Dept. of Anthropology 2004)

Web page	References
	Cited
		Harvard University, Department of Anthropology
		    2004 Graduate Program. Web page. Electronic
		        document, http://www.fas.harvard.edu/
		        ~anthro/graduate_program.html,
		        accessed November 30, 2004.

	In-text	(Harvard University, Dept. of Anthropology Graduate Program 2004)

Weblog,
entry or
comment
	References
	Cited
		Drezner, Daniel
		    2005 The EU Needs to Turn the Key. Weblog
		        posting. October 23. Electronic document,
		        http://www.danieldrezner.com/blog/,
		        accessed October 24, 2005.
		Xiong, Joshua
		    2005 Comment: The EU needs to turn the key.
		        Weblog comment. October 23. Electronic
		        document, http://www.danieldrezner
		        .com/mt/mt-comments.cgi?entry_id=2370,
		        accessed October 24, 2005.
		Ideas Bazaar: Anthropology and Ethnography
		    2004 Immigration and the Savage Mind.
		        Weblog posting. November 4. Electronic
		        document, http://www.ideasbazaar.com/
		        blog/archives/cats/anthropology_and_et
		        .php, accessed November 30, 2004.

	In-text	(Drezner 2004) (Xiong 2005) (Ideas Bazaar 2004)

7 CSE CITATIONS FOR THE BIOLOGICAL SCIENCES

CSE citations, devised by the Council of Science Editors, are widely used for scientific papers, journals, and books in the life sciences. The citations are based on international principles adopted by the National Library of Medicine.

Actually, the CSE system lets you choose among three ways of citing documents:

- *Citation-sequence:* Citations are numbered (1), (2), (3), in the order they appear in the text. Full references appear at the end of the paper—in the same order. They are *not* alphabetized.
- *Citation-name:* Citations are numbered, with full references at the end of the paper—in alphabetical order. The first item cited in the text might be number eight on the alphabetical list. It would be cited as (8), even though it appeared first—and (8) if it appears again.
- *Name-year:* Citations in the text are given as name and year, such as (McClintock 2006). Full references appear at the end of the paper in alphabetical order, just as they do in APA citations.

Whichever format you choose, use it consistently throughout the paper. Ask your instructor which one she prefers.

Citation-sequence: Cite the first reference in the text as number 1, the second as number 2, and so on. You can use brackets [1], superscripts[1], or parentheses (1). At the end of the paper, list all the items, beginning with the first one cited. The list is *not* alphabetical. If the first item you cite is by Professor Zangwill, then that's the first item in the reference list. If you cite Zangwill's paper again, it's still [1], even if it's the last citation in your paper. If you want to cite several items at once, simply include the number for each one, separated by commas, such as [1,3,9] or [1,3,9] or (1,3,9). If items have successive numbers, use hyphens: 4-6,12-18.

Citation-name: Begin by assembling an alphabetical list of references at the end of the text and numbering them. Each item in the list will have a number, which is used whenever that book or article is cited in the text. If the Zangwill article is thirty-sixth in the alphabetical list, then it is always cited with that number, even if it's the first item you cite in the paper. The next reference in the text might be [23], the one after that might be [12]. Citations can be set as superscripts, in brackets, or in parentheses. If you want to cite several items at once, include a number for each one, such as [4,15,22] or [4,15,22] or (4,15,22). Use hyphens for continuous numbers (1-3). So a citation could be (4,16-18,22).

Name-year: For in-text citations, use the (name-year) format without commas, such as (Cronin and Siegler 2005) and (Siegler and others 2006). The reference list is alphabetical by author and includes all cited articles. If an author has several articles, list the earliest ones first. Follow the same method if an author has published several articles in the same year. List the first one as 2006a, the second as 2006b, and so on by the month of publication. To cite several articles by Susan Lindquist, then, the notation might be (Lindquist 2003d, 2004a, 2004h), referring to those three articles in the reference list.

In the same way, you can also cite articles by different authors within the same reference. Separate them by semicolons, such as (Liebman 2001; Ma and Lindquist 2003; Outeiro and Lindquist 2003).

If the author's name appears in the sentence, you do not need to repeat it in the citation. For example, "According to LaBarbera (2006), this experiment..."

What if LaBarbera had ten or fifteen coauthors? That's certainly possible in the sciences. Articles sometimes have dozens of authors because they include everyone involved in the experiments leading to publication. My colleague Henry Frisch, a high-energy physicist, told me that one of his articles has nearly eight hundred coauthors![1] I grew up in a town with a smaller phone book. Really.

How many of these authors should you include when you use name-year citations in the text? Don't go overboard. Just list the first seven hundred. If

---

1. Professor Frisch's own practice is to list himself as author only if he actually helped write the paper. His practice is unusual, but a number of scientists think he's right and that current practices are unclear and often lax. To correct the problem, some scientists are circulating proposals that would require coauthors to specify how they contributed to joint papers. For Frisch's comments on the metastasizing growth of coauthors, see his Web page, http://hep.uchicago.edu/~frisch.

you do that in the first sentence, you'll reach the paper's word limit before you even have to write a second sentence. That's one easy science paper.

Actually, CSE offers clear recommendations, stopping a bit short of seven hundred authors. If there are only two authors, list them both, separated by "and." If there are three or more authors, list only the first one, followed by "and others." For example: (LaBarbera and others 2004). Notice, by the way, that CSE uses the English phrase "and others" rather than the Latin "et al.," used in most other citation styles. Later, I'll show you how to handle coauthors in the reference list at the end of the paper.

QUICK COMPARISON OF CSE STYLES

Style	In-text citations	Reference list at end of paper
Citation-sequence	(1), (2), (3), (4)	Items listed in order of their text appearance
Citation-name	(31), (2), (13), (7)	Items listed alphabetically, by author surname
Name-year	(Shapiro 2004)	Items listed alphabetically, by author surname

STYLES OF REFERENCE LISTS

All three styles require reference lists following the text. CSE emphasizes brevity and simplicity for these lists. Instead of using the authors' first names, use only their initials. Omit periods after the initials and don't put spaces between them: Stern HK. Shorten journal names with standard abbreviations, such as those given in the *Index Medicus* system, available online at http://www.nlm.nih.gov/tsd/serials/lji.html.

CSE uses sentence-style capitalization for titles. Capitalize only the first word, proper nouns, and the first word after a colon. Print the titles in normal type rather than italics. Hanging indents are optional.

If you cite something you've read online rather than in print, cite the electronic version. After all, the two versions may differ. To do that, CSE style requires you to add a couple of items to the citation: (1) the date you accessed the document and (2) the fact that it was an Internet document. With CSE style, you need to show when you accessed the article. That comes in brackets after the publication date. You also need to show that you are citing the electronic version. To do that, simply add [Internet] in square brackets, immediately after the journal title.

Print citation	Jacob S, McClintock MK, Zelano B, Ober C. 2002. Paternally inherited HLA alleles are associated with women's choice of male odor. Nat Genet 30:175–9.
Internet citation	Jacob S, McClintock MK, Zelano B, Ober C. 2002 [cited 2004 Feb 2]. Paternally inherited HLA alleles are associated with women's choice of male odor. Nat Genet [Internet]; 30:175–9.

If you wish to include the URL for the article, put it after the page numbers. If there is a document identification number (DOI) or other database number, put it last. There is no period after the DOI.

Internet citation with URL and document ID number	Jacob S, McClintock MK, Zelano B, Ober C. 2002 [cited 2004 Feb 2]. Paternally inherited HLA alleles are associated with women's choice of male odor. Nat Genet [Internet]; 30:175–9. Available from: http://genes.uchicago.edu/ fri/jacob_ober5.pdf. DOI: 10.1038/ng830

This article, like nearly all printed articles, was not modified after it was published. But preprints are often modified and so are articles in electronic journals. You need to include that information in the citation so your readers will know which version you are citing. That information appears in the square brackets, immediately before the date you accessed the item.

Modified paper	Jacob S, McClintock MK, Zelano B, Ober C. 2002 [modified 2004 Jan 20; cited 2004 Feb 2]. Paternally inherited HLA alleles are associated with women's choice of male odor. Nat Genet [Internet]; 30:175–9. Available from: http://genes.uchicago.edu/fri/jacob_ober5.pdf. DOI: 10.1038/ng830

Don't worry about remembering all these details. There are too many of them. I'll explain them in the tables that follow and include plenty of examples. If you use this style often, you'll gradually grow familiar with the fine points.

These tables show CSE recommendations for in-text citations and reference lists, using all three formats. Not every journal follows them exactly, so you'll see some variation as you read scientific publications. Journals differ, for example, in how many coauthors they include in the reference list. Some list only the first three authors before adding "and others." One lists the first twenty-six. (Imagine being poor coauthor number 27.) The CSE recommends naming up to ten and then adding "and others."

These tables are based on the forthcoming seventh edition of the CSE style manual.

CSE: NAME-YEAR SYSTEM

Journal article	Reference list	Zhang S, Sha Q, Chen HS, Dong J, Jiang R. 2003. Transmission/disequilibrium test based on haplotype sharing for tightly linked markers. Am J Hum Genet 73(3):566–79.
	In-text	(Zhang and others 2003) ▸ If your list includes several publications by Zhang in 2003, your in-text reference should include coauthors to clarify exactly which article you are citing. For example: (Zhang, Sha and others 2003).
Journal article, online	Reference list	Bhandari V. 2003 [cited 2004 Jan 2]. The role of nitric oxide in hyperoxia-induced injury to the developing lung. Front Biosci [Internet];8:e361–9. Available from: http://www.bioscience.org/2003/v8/e/1086/list.htm ▸ This journal article is online only. Do *not* add a period at the end of the URL.
	In-text	(Bhandari 2003)
Book, one author	Reference list	Kardong KV. 2002. Vertebrates: Comparative anatomy, function, evolution. New York: McGraw-Hill. ▸ If the publisher's city is well known, you may omit the state.

	In-text	(Kardong 2002)
		▶ To cite the same author for works written in several years:
		(Kardong 1996, 2000, 2002a, 2002b)
		▶ To cite works by authors with the same surname published in the same year, include the authors' initials:
		(Kardong KV 2002; Kardong LS 2002)
Book, multiple authors	Reference list	Kohane IS, Kho AT, Butte AJ. 2003. Microarrays for an integrative genomics. Cambridge (MA): MIT Press.
		▶ In the reference list, name up to ten authors, then add "and others."
	In-text	(Kohane and others 2003)
		▶ If there are just two authors, name them both:
		(Kohane and Kho 1995)
Book, multiple editions	Reference list	Snell RS. 2004. Clinical anatomy. 7th ed. Philadelphia: Lippincott Williams & Wilkins.
		▶ For a revised edition, the phrase "Rev. ed." appears where "7th ed." currently does.
	In-text	(Snell 2004)
Book, multiple editions, no author	Reference list	Publication manual of the American Psychological Association. 2001. 5th ed. Washington (DC): American Psychological Association.
	In-text	(Publication manual ... 2001)
		▶ Do not use "Anonymous" in place of the author name. Instead, use the first word or first few words of the title and an ellipsis, followed by the date.

Book, edited	Reference list	Marr JJ, Nilsen TW, Komuniecki RW, editors. 2003. Molecular medical parasitology. Amsterdam (Netherlands): Academic Press.
	In-text	(Marr and others 2003)
Chapter in edited book	Reference list	Kramer JA. 2003. Overview of the tools for microarray analysis: Transcription profiling, DNA chips, and differential display. In: Krawetz SA, Womble DD, editors. Introduction to bioinformatics: A theoretical and practical approach. Totowa (NJ): Humana Press. Pp. 637–63.
	In-text	(Kramer 2003)
Government document	Reference list	[NHLBI] National Heart, Lung, and Blood Institute (US), National High Blood Pressure Education Program. 2003 [cited 2003 Oct 12]. The seventh report of the Joint National Committee on Prevention, Detection, Evaluation, and Treatment of High Blood Pressure (JNC7) [Internet]. Bethesda (MD): National Heart, Lung, and Blood Institute (US). Available from: http://www.nhlbi.nih.gov/guidelines/hypertension/index.htm ▶ If an organization is both author and publisher, the name may be abbreviated as publisher. For example, Bethesda (MD): The Institute.
	In-text	(NHLBI 2003)
Database	Reference list	[PDB] Protein Data Bank. 2004 [cited 2004 Jan 5]. Available from: http://www.rcsb.org/pdb/
	In-text	(Protein Data Bank 2004) or (PDB 2004)

Internet	Reference list	[CSF] Council of Science Editors. 2003 [cited 2003 Oct 12]. Citing the Internet: Formats for bibliographic citation [Internet]. Reston (VA): Council of Science Editors. Available from: http://www.councilscienceeditors .org/publications/citing_internet.cfm ▸ Where this citation says only [Internet], yours might say [monograph on Internet] or [database on Internet].
	In-text	(CSE 2003)

The next table shows CSE references using citation-sequence and citation-name formats. The main difference from the previous table is that the date appears later in the reference. The list does not use hanging indents. I have used the same articles, in case you want to compare formats.

CSE: CITATION-SEQUENCE AND CITATION-NAME SYSTEMS

Journal article	Reference list	Zhang S, Sha Q, Chen HS, Dong J, Jiang R. Transmission/disequilibrium test based on haplotype sharing for tightly linked markers. Am J Hum Genet 2003;73(3):566–79.
Journal article, online	Reference list	Bhandari V. The role of nitric oxide in hyperoxia-induced injury to the developing lung. Front Biosci [Internet] 2003 [cited 2004 Jan 2];8:e361–9. Available from: http://www.bioscience.org/2003/v8/e/ 1086/list.htm ▸ This journal article is online only.
Book, one author	Reference list	Kardong KV. Vertebrates: Comparative anatomy, function, evolution. New York: McGraw-Hill; 2002. ▸ If the publisher's city is well known, you may omit the state abbreviation, if you wish.

Book, multiple authors	Reference list	Kohane IS, Kho AT, Butte AJ. Microarrays for an integrative genomics. Cambridge (MA): MIT Press; 2003. ▶ In the reference list, name up to ten authors, then add "and others."
Book, multiple editions	Reference list	Snell RS. Clinical anatomy. 7th ed. Philadelphia: Lippincott Williams & Wilkins; 2004. ▶ For a revised edition, use "Rev. ed." in place of "7th ed."
Book, multiple editions, no author	Reference list	Publication manual of the American Psychological Association. 5th ed. Washington (DC): American Psychological Association; 2001.
Book, edited	Reference list	Marr JJ, Nilsen TW, Komuniecki RW, editors. Molecular medical parasitology. Amsterdam (Netherlands): Academic Press; 2003.
Chapter in edited book	Reference list	Kramer JA. Overview of the tools for microarray analysis: Transcription profiling, DNA chips, and differential display. In: Krawetz SA, Womble DD, editors. Introduction to bioinformatics: A theoretical and practical approach. Totowa (NJ): Humana Press; 2003. Pp. 637–63.
Government document	Reference list	National Heart, Lung, and Blood Institute (US), National High Blood Pressure Education Program. The seventh report of the Joint National Committee on Prevention, Detection, Evaluation, and Treatment of High Blood Pressure (JNC7) [Internet]. Bethesda (MD): National Heart, Lung, and Blood Institute (US); 2003 [cited 2003 Oct 12].

		Available from: http://www.nhlbi.nih.gov/ guidelines/hypertension/index.htm
Database	Reference list	Protein Data Bank (PDB). 2004 [cited 2004 Jan 5]. Available from: http://www.rcsb.org/pdb/
Internet	Reference list	Council of Science Editors. Citing the Internet: Formats for bibliographic citation [Internet]. Reston (VA): Council of Science Editors; 2003 [cited 2003 Oct 12]. Available http://www .councilscienceeditors.org/ publications/citing_internet.cfm
		National Library of Medicine. Recommended formats for bibliographic citation, supplement: Internet formats [Internet]. 2001 [cited 2004 Jan 5]. Available from: http:// www.nlm.nih.gov/pubs/formats/internet.pdf
		▶ Where this citation says [Internet], yours might say [monograph on Internet] or [database on Internet].

Although individual references (shown above) are the same for both the citation-sequence and citation-name systems, their full reference lists are compiled in different orders.

Order of items within reference lists:

- Citation-name system: alphabetical by author
- Citation-sequence system: order of first appearance in the text

To illustrate, let's take the opening sentence of an article and show how each style would handle the citations and reference list.

CSE: CITATION-SEQUENCE SYSTEM (ILLUSTRATION OF REFERENCE LIST ORDER)

Opening
sentence

This research deals with the ABC transporter family and builds on prior studies by Zeleznikar and others,[1] Randak and Welsh,[2] and Dean and others.[3]

Reference list
(in order of
appearance in
text)

[1] Zeleznikar RJ, Dzeja PP, Goldberg, ND. Adenylate kinase-catalyzed phosphoryl transfer couples ATP utilization with its generation by glycolysis in intact muscle. J Biol Chem 1995;270(13):7311–9. PMID: 7706272

[2] Randak C, Welsh MJ. An intrinsic adenylate kinase activity regulates gating of the ABC transporter CFTR. Cell [Internet]. 2003 [cited 2003 Oct 12];115(7):837–50. PMID: 14697202

[3] Dean M, Rzhetsky A, Allikmets R. The human ATP-binding cassette (ABC) transporter superfamily. Genome Res [Internet]. 2001 [cited 2001 Apr 3];11(7):1156–66. PMID: 11435397

▶ Zeleznikar's article is listed first because it is the first one mentioned in the text.

CSE: CITATION-NAME SYSTEM (ILLUSTRATION OF REFERENCE LIST ORDER)

Opening
sentence

This research deals with the ABC transporter family and builds on prior studies by Zeleznikar and others,[3] Randak and Welsh,[2] and Dean and others.[1]

Reference list
(alphabetical)

[1] Dean M, Rzhetsky A, Allikmets R. The human ATP-binding cassette (ABC) transporter superfamily. Genome Res [Internet]. 2001 [cited 2001 Apr 3];11(7):1156–66. PMID: 11435397

[2] Randak C, Welsh MJ. An intrinsic adenylate kinase activity regulates gating of the ABC transporter CFTR. Cell [Internet]. 2003 [cited 2003 Oct 12];115(7):837–50. PMID: 14697202

[3] Zeleznikar RJ, Dzeja PP, Goldberg ND. Adenylate kinase-catalyzed phosphoryl transfer couples ATP utilization with its generation by glycolysis in intact muscle. J Biol Chem 1995;270(13):7311–9. PMID: 7706272

▶ Zeleznikar's article is listed last because it is last alphabetically.

The two systems, citation sequence and citation-name, present *each item* in the reference list the same way. What's different are (1) the *order* of items in the reference list and (2) their *citation numbers* in the text.

There's one more item you may wish to include in your citations: the PMID number. All medical articles have this electronic tag, which identifies them within the comprehensive PubMed database. The PMID appears as the last item in the citation and is *not* followed by a period:

Dean M, Rzhetsky A, Allikmets R. The human ATP-binding cassette (ABC) transporter superfamily. Genome Res [Internet]. 2001 [cited 2001 Apr 3];11(7):1156–66. PMID: 11435397

The PubMed database, covering more than four thousand biomedical journals, was developed at the National Library of Medicine and is available online at www.ncbi.nlm.nih.gov/entrez.

Detailed information about CSE citations for the sciences can be found in

- *Scientific Style and Format: The CBE Manual for Authors, Editors, and Publishers*, 6th ed. (Cambridge: Cambridge University Press; 1994). Published for the Council of Biology Editors, now renamed the Council of Science Editors.

The sixth edition covers citations in two styles: name-date and citation-sequence. The upcoming seventh edition adds citation-name. This chapter conforms to the forthcoming edition, thanks to the generous assistance of two scholars working on the new volume: Peggy Robinson (chair of the CSE's Style Manual Subcommittee) and Karen J. Patrias (of the National Library of Medicine, Reference Section).

8 AMA CITATIONS FOR THE BIOMEDICAL SCIENCES, MEDICINE, AND NURSING

AMA citations are used in biomedical research, medicine, nursing, and some related fields of biology. They are based on the *American Medical Association Manual of Style: A Guide for Authors and Editors*, 9th ed. (Baltimore, MD: Williams & Wilkins, 1998).

Citations are numbered (1), (2), (3), in the order they appear in the text. Full references appear at the end of the paper—in the same order. For coauthored books and articles, you should list up to six authors. If there are more, list only the first three, followed by "et al." Rather than using the authors' first names, use their initials (without periods) and do not put spaces between the initials: Lipson CH. Abbreviate the title of journals. There's a standard list of abbreviations (the *Index Medicus* system) available online at http://www.nlm.nih.gov/tsd/serials/lji.html.

AMA CITATIONS

Journal article	Cooper DS. Hyperthyroidism. *Lancet.* 2003;362:459–468.
	Cummings JL, Cole G. Alzheimer disease. *JAMA.* 2002;287:2335–2338.
	Beinart SC, Sales AE, Spertus JA, Plomondon ME, Every NR, Rumsfeld JS. Impact of angina burden and other factors on treatment satisfaction after acute coronary syndromes. *Am Heart J.* 2003;146:646–652.
	▸ Name up to six authors in articles or books. If there are more, name the first three, then use "et al." This article, for example, has thirteen listed authors:
	Wen G, Mahata SK, Cadman P, et al. Both rare and common polymorphisms contribute functional variation at CHGA, a regulator of catecholamine physiology. *Am J Hum Genet.* 2004;74:197–207.

> ▸ Journal titles are abbreviated without periods. (There is a period after "*Genet.*" only because it is the last word in the journal's title.) Likewise, there is a period after "et al" only because a period always follows the final author's name.

Journal article, online	Bhandari V. The role of nitric oxide in hyperoxia-induced injury to the developing lung. *Front Biosci* [serial online]. 2003;8:e361–e369. Available from: http://www .bioscience.org/2003/v8/e/1086/list.htm. Accessed October 12, 2003. ▸ This journal article is online only.
Unpublished material or preprint	Shankar RP, Partha P, Shenoy NK, and Brahmadathan KN. Investigation of antimicrobial use pattern in the intensive treatment unit of a teaching hospital in western Nepal. Preprint. July 26, 2002. Clinmed/2002050008. Available at: http://clinmed.netprints.org/cgi/content/full/ 2002050008v1. Accessed March 7, 2004.
Published letter or comment	Hecht H, Rumberger JA, Budoff MJ. C-reactive protein and electron beam tomography [letter]. *Circulation*. 2003;107:e123–e124.
Book, one author	Krimsky S. *Science in the Private Interest: Has the Lure of Profits Corrupted Biomedical Research?* Lanham, Md: Rowman & Littlefield; 2003. ▸ Notice how the state name is abbreviated. Beasley RW. *Beasley's Surgery of the Hand.* New York, NY: Thieme; 2003.
Book, multiple authors	Marso SP, Stern DM. *Diabetes and Cardiovascular Disease: Integrating Science and Clinical Medicine.* Philadelphia, Pa: Lippincott Williams & Wilkins; 2003.
Book, multiple editions	Snell RS. *Clinical Anatomy.* 7th ed. Philadelphia, Pa: Lippincott Williams & Wilkins; 2004. Brown MA, Semelka RC. *MRI: Basic Principles and Applications.* 3rd ed. Hoboken, NJ: Wiley-Liss; 2003.

Book, multiple editions (*continued*)	▶ The edition number appears between the book's title and the place of publication. ▶ For a revised edition, use "Rev. ed." in place of the specific edition.
Book, multiple editions, no author	*Dorland's Illustrated Medical Dictionary.* 30th ed. Philadelphia, Pa: Saunders; 2003. *Nursing 2004 Drug Handbook.* 24th ed. Springhouse, Pa: Springhouse; 2003.
Reference book	Juo P-S. *Concise Dictionary of Biomedicine and Molecular Biology.* 2nd ed. Boca Raton, Fla: CRC Press; 2001. Dox IG, Melloni BJ. *Melloni's Illustrated Medical Dictionary.* 4th ed. London, Eng: Parthenon Publishing; 2002. Fuster V, Alexander RW, O'Rourke RA, eds. *Hurst's The Heart.* Vol 2. 10th ed. New York, NY: McGraw Hill; 2002. ▶ "Vol" does not have a period. AMA eliminates periods after abbreviations.
Book, edited	Marr JJ, Nilsen TW, Komuniecki RW, eds. *Molecular Medical Parasitology.* Amsterdam, Neth: Academic Press; 2003.
Chapter in edited book	Kramer JA. Overview of the tools for microarray analysis: Transcription profiling, DNA chips, and differential display. In: Krawetz SA, Womble DD, eds. *Introduction to Bioinformatics: A Theoretical and Practical Approach.* Totowa, NJ: Humana Press; 2003:637–663.
Government document	Agency for Healthcare Research and Quality. *Ephedra and Ephedrine for Weight Loss and Athletic Performance Enhancement: Clinical Efficacy and Side Effects.* Washington, DC: US Dept of Health and Human Services; 2001.

National Heart, Lung, and Blood Institute (US), National High Blood Pressure Education Program. *The Seventh Report of the Joint National Committee on Prevention, Detection, Evaluation, and Treatment of High Blood Pressure* (JNC7) [Internet]. Bethesda, Md: National Heart, Lung, and Blood Institute (US); 2003. Available at: http://www.nhlbi.nih.gov/guidelines/hypertension/index.htm. Accessed November 12, 2003.

Personal comment, untitled lecture, or informal communication	Mass DP. Lecture on hand surgery. February 2, 2006. ▸ Using AMA style, your reference list may include lectures and public talks, but not personal communications such as letters and private discussions.
CD-ROM or DVD	Amiel S, Mukharjee A, Aitken V. *Essentials in Endocrinology III: Diabetes* [CD-ROM]. London, Eng: Royal Society of Medicine Press; 2002. National Library of Medicine. *Changing the Face of Medicine* [interviews on DVD]. Washington, DC: Friends of the National Library of Medicine; 2004.
Database	Protein Data Bank [database online]. Available at: http://www.rcsb.org/pdb/. Accessed January 28, 2004. National Center for Health Statistics. NHIS 2002 data release. Available at: ftp://ftp.cdc.gov/pub/Health_Statistics/NCHS/Datasets/NHIS/2002/. Accessed January 28, 2004.
Internet	US Preventive Services Task Force, Agency for Healthcare Research and Quality Web site. Screening for Prostate Cancer: Recommendations and Rationale. Available at: http://www.ahrq.gov/clinic/3rduspstf/prostatescr/prostaterr.htm. Accessed January 28, 2004.

To illustrate how these citations appear in the text, let's take the opening sentence of an article.

AMA (ILLUSTRATION OF REFERENCE LIST ORDER)

Opening sentence	This research deals with the ABC transporter family and builds on prior studies by Zeleznikar et al,[1] Randak and Welsh,[2] and Dean et al.[3]
Reference list (in order of appearance in text)	[1] Zeleznikar RJ, Dzeja PP, Goldberg, ND. Adenylate kinase-catalyzed phosphoryl transfer couples ATP utilization with its generation by glycolysis in intact muscle. *J Biol Chem.*1995;270(13):7311–7319.
	[2] Randak C, Welsh MJ. An intrinsic adenylate kinase activity regulates gating of the ABC transporter CFTR. *Cell* [Internet]. 2003;115(7):837–850.
	[3] Dean M, Rzhetsky A, Allikmets, R. The human ATP-binding cassette (ABC) transporter superfamily. *Genome Res* [Internet]. 2001;11(7):1156–1166.
	► Zeleznikar's article is listed first because it is the first one mentioned in the text. Notice that "et al" does not include a period when it is used in sentences, according to AMA style.

Finally, all medical articles have an electronic identification number, known as a PMID. You are not required to include it, but it often helps your readers. It will help you, too, if you need to return to the article. The PMID appears as the last item in the citation and is followed by a period:

> Randak C, Welsh MJ. An intrinsic adenylate kinase activity regulates gating of the ABC transporter CFTR. *Cell* [Internet]. 2003;115(7): 837–850. PMID: 14697202.

The PMID identifies the document within the PubMed database, which includes virtually all biomedical journals. This database was developed at the National Library of Medicine and it is available online at www.ncbi.nlm.nih.gov/entrez.

9 ACS CITATIONS FOR CHEMISTRY

The American Chemical Society (ACS) has its own style guide, which gives you a choice of citation formats:

- In-text citations with name and year, similar to APA or CSE. The reference list is alphabetized and appears at the end of the paper.
- Numbered citations, with a reference list at the end of the paper. End references are numbered in the order they appear in the text. These numbered citations, as they appear in the text itself, are either
  - superscript, such as[23], or
  - parenthesis with the number in italics, such as (*23*).

Each format is used by scores of chemistry journals. Your lab, instructor, or journal may prefer one over the other. Whichever one you choose, use it consistently throughout each paper.

Fortunately, you collect the same information for either format. In fact, the items in the reference list are presented exactly the same way, whether the list is numbered or alphabetized.

- The author's last name appears first, followed by a comma and then initials (instead of given names), such as Fenn, J. B. Initials are followed by periods.
- Instead of "page," the reference list uses "p" and "pp" without periods.
- For books
  - Include the title and italicize it. That's true for edited books, too.
  - Put the publisher's name before the location, as in CRC Press: Boca Raton, FL.
  - Include the year of publication, using normal typeface, such as Wiley-Interscience: New York, 2004.
  - Show pagination in books by using "pp"—for example: CRC Press: Boca Raton, FL, 2004; pp 507–15.

- For edited books, you may include (or omit) the titles of specific chapters; just be consistent.

- For journals
  - Include the journal title, abbreviated and italicized, such as *J. Am. Chem. Soc.*
  - Include the year of publication in **boldface,** the volume number in italics, and the first page number (or total pages) of the article in normal type, such as *Org. Lett.* **2004,** *3*, 215.
  - Show pagination in articles *without* using "pp"—for example: *Chem. Eng. News.* **2004,** *82*, 39–40.
  - Omit titles of journal articles.

There is no explanation for these mysterious details. My guess: the chemists were overcome by fumes many years ago, and the odd results are now beloved traditions.

ACS (CHEMISTRY): REFERENCE LIST AND IN-TEXT CITATIONS

Journal article	Reference list	Zhao, S.; Liao, X.; Cook, J. M. *Org. Lett.* **2002,** *4*, 687. ▸ Article title is always omitted. ▸ Year of publication is in boldface; volume number is italicized. ▸ Journal titles are italicized and abbreviated according to the *Chemical Abstracts Service Source Index* (CASSI).
	In-text	(Zhao et al., 2002)
Journal article, online	Reference list	Wilson, E. *Chem. Eng. News* [Online]. **2003,** *81*, 35–36.
	In-text	(Wilson, 2003)

Chemical abstract	Reference list	Taneda, A.; Shimizu, T.; Kawazoe, Y. *J. Phys.:* *Condens. Matter* **2001**, *13(16)*, L305–312 (Eng.); *Chem. Abstr.* **2001**, *134*, 372018a. ▶ This article by Taneda was published in a journal and referenced in *Chemical Abstracts*. This citation shows a reference to both the full article and the abstract. The abstract always comes second and is separated from the article by a semicolon. Taneda, A.; Shimizu, T.; Kawazoe, Y. *Chem.* *Abstr.* **2001**, *134*, 372018a. ▶ Same article but shown only as mentioned in *Chemical Abstracts*. It is better to refer to the full published article than the abstract, but that requires you actually examine the full article. *Chem. Abstr.* **2001**, *134*, 372018a. ▶ This is the same article, referred to solely by its *Chemical Abstract* number. That number—*134*, 372018a—is the CAS accession number. The number *134* is the volume and 372018a is the abstract number in the print version of *Chemical Abstracts*. ▶ In some earlier editions of *Chemical Abstracts*, there are several abstracts per page. Abstract f on page 1167 can be cited as 1167*f* (or 1167[f]). ▶ It is usually better to include the authors, as in the previous references to Taneda et al.
	In-text	(Taneda et al., 2001) (*Chem. Abstr.*, 2001)
Book, one author	Reference list	Eberhardt, M. K. *Reactive Oxygen Metabolites:* *Chemistry and Medical Consequences*. CRC Press: Boca Raton, FL, 2001; pp 23–42. ▶ Or: chapter 3 instead of the pagination.
	In-text	(Eberhardt, 2001)

Book, multiple authors	Reference list	Buncel, E.; Dust, J. M. *Carbanion Chemistry: Structures and Mechanisms*. American Chemical Society: Washington, DC, 2003. ▸ *What if there are many authors? The ACS Style Guide* says to name them all. It also notes that some chemistry journals list only the first ten, followed by a semicolon and "et al."
	In-text	(Buncel and Dust, 2003) ▸ Include up to two names for in-text citations. If there are three or more, use this form: (Buncel et al., 2003)
Book, multiple editions	Reference list	Sorenson, W. R.; Sweeny, W.; Campbell, T. W. *Preparative Methods of Polymer Chemistry*, 3rd ed.; Wiley-Interscience: New York, 2001. ▸ For a revised edition, use "Rev. ed." instead of "3rd ed."
	In-text	(Sorenson et al., 2001)
Book multiple editions, no author	Reference list	*McGraw-Hill Encyclopedia of Science and Technology*, 9th ed.; McGraw-Hill: New York, 2002; 20 vols.
	In-text	(McGraw-Hill, 2002) ▸ To cite a particular volume: (McGraw-Hill, vol. 6, 2002)
Book, multivolume	Reference list	Shore, B. W. *The Theory of Coherent Atomic Excitation: Multilevel Atoms and Incoherence*. Wiley: New York, 1990; Vol. 2.
	In-text	(Shore, vol. 2, 1990)
Book, edited	Reference list	*Oxidative Delignification Chemistry: Fundamentals and Catalysis*; Argyropoulos, D. S., Ed.; American Chemical Society: Washington, DC, 2001.
	In-text	(Argyropoulos, 2001)

Chapter in edited book	Reference list	Wilson, S. R., et al. In *Fullerenes: Chemistry, Physics, and Technology*; Kadish, K. M., Ruoff, R. S., Eds.; Wiley-Interscience: New York, 2000; pp 91–176.

▶ Or

Wilson, S. R.; Schuster, D. I.; Nuber, B.; Meier, M. S.; Maggini, M.; Prato, M.; Taylor, R. In *Fullerenes: Chemistry, Physics, and Technology*; Kadish, K. M., Ruoff, R. S., Eds.; Wiley-Interscience: New York, 2000; pp 91–176.

▶ You may include or omit the chapter title; just be consistent.

▶ How many authors should you list? If there are only two, list both (Jones and Smith). If there are more, the *ACS Style Guide* says to list them as (Jones et al.). In practice, many chemical journals list up to nine or ten authors; for larger numbers, they list only the first author plus "et al."

	In-text	(Wilson et al., 2000)

▶ Normally use only one or two names for in-text citations. Occasionally, though, you will find top chemistry journals citing more authors, such as:

(Wilson, Schuster, Nuber, Meier, Maggini, Prato, Taylor, 2000)

Conference paper	Reference list	Haskard, C. A.; Schaupt, I.; Weller, M. G. Presented at the Xth International Conference on Harmful Algae, St. Pete Beach, FL, October 2002; Poster.
	In-text	(Haskard, Schaupt, Weller, 2002)

Government document	Reference list	Substance Abuse and Mental Health Services Administration. *Keeping Youth Drug Free.* DHHS Publication No. (SMA) 3772; Center for Substance Abuse Prevention: Rockville, MD, 2003. Supplemental Environmental Impact Statement for the Airborne Laser Program. *Fed. Regist.* **2003**, *68* (163), 50756–50760. ▸ The *Federal Register* is treated like a journal.
	In-text	(*Keeping Youth Drug Free*, 2003)
Patent	Reference list	Searle, R. G. Carbon Dioxide Recovery in an Ethylene to Ethylene Oxide Production Process. U.S. Patent 6495609, 2002. ▸ It is also acceptable to omit the name of the patent.
	In-text	(Searle, 2002)
CD-ROM or DVD	Reference list	Luceigh, B. A. *Chem TV: Organic Chemistry* 3.0 [CD-ROM], 2004.
	In-text	(Luceigh, 2004)
Internet	Reference list	Biochemical Periodic Tables. http://umbbd.ahc.umn.edu/periodic/links.html (accessed Jan 2004). ▸ If the page has an author, his name and initial appear before the title of the page: Oxtoby, J. Biochemical Periodic Tables. http://. . .
	In-text	(Oxtoby, 2004)

Detailed information on ACS citations is available in

• Janet S. Dodd, ed., *The ACS Style Guide: A Manual for Authors and Editors*, 2nd ed. (Washington, DC: American Chemical Society, 1997).

10 PHYSICS, ASTROPHYSICS, AND ASTRONOMY CITATIONS

AIP CITATIONS IN PHYSICS

Physics citations are based on the *AIP Style Manual*, 4th ed. (New York: American Institute of Physics, 1990). Most physics journals use numbered citations in the text. Items appear in the numbered reference list in the order they appear in the text. The items are not indented. (A few physics journals use the author-year style instead. It has an alphabetized reference list with hanging indents.)

Whichever format is used, individual items in the reference list look the same, at least for articles and preprints (which are the way researchers communicate). References are brief: Authors' names (M. Shochet and S. Nagel), abbreviated journal title, **boldface number for the journal volume**, first page number of the article, and, finally, the year in parentheses.

AIP (PHYSICS): REFERENCE LIST

Journal article

[1] D. Groom et al., Euro. Phys. J. C **15**, 1 (2000).

[2] J. Wisdom, Nucl. Phys. B **2** (Proc. Suppl.), **391** (1987).

- ▸ The article's title is always omitted. Journal titles are abbreviated and not italicized.
- ▸ The publication volume (or issue number) and series are in boldface. For example, if a reference is to an article in *Physical Letters B*, issue number 466, page 415, then it appears as Phys. Lett. B **466**, 415 (1999).

Journal article, online

[#] Y. Nakayama and S. Akita, New J. Phys. **5**, 128 (2003). <http://ej.iop.org/links/57/Hd+yfNDozFMnm2H8QoyUKA/njp3_1_128.pdf>.

- ▸ This is an online-only journal.

Journal article, online (*continued*)	▸ The citation may also include a DOI or PII after the URL. DOI is a digital object identifier. PII is a publisher item identifier. Both are ways of uniquely identifying electronic documents. For the Nakayama and Akita article, DOI: 10.1088/1367-2630/5/1/128; PII: S1367-2630(03)65453-4.
	▸ Online articles are referenced the same way as articles in print, except that they may include an electronic article number (if one is available), instead of this issue and page number. Example: Phys. Rev. B **63**, 012013 (2001).
Preprint	[#] F. Zantow, O. Kaczmarek, F. Karsch, P. Petreczky, preprint, hep-lat/0301015 (2003). ⟨http://www.thphys.uni-heidelberg.de/hep-lat/0301.html⟩.
	[#] A. J. M. Medved, preprint, hep-th/0301010J (2003). ⟨http://arxiv.org/abs/hep-th/0301010⟩. Published in High Energy Phys. **5**, 008 (2003). ⟨http://www.iop.org/EJ/abstract/1126-6708/2003/05/008/⟩.
	▸ hep-th = Heidelberg High Energy Physics Preprint Service, e-prints on theoretical physics; hep-lat = e-prints on lattices.
Book, one author	[#] P. Phillips, *Advanced Solid State Physics* (Westview, Boulder, CO, 2003).
Book, multiple authors	[#] J. E. Marsden and T. S. Ratiu, *Introduction to Mechanics and Symmetry* (Springer, New York, 1994).
	▸ The *AIP Style Manual* does not say how many authors you should list. If the list is long, however, name only the first and add "et al." Example: Marsden et al., *Introduction . . .*
Book, multiple editions	[#] G. Börner, *The Early Universe*, 4th ed. (Springer, Berlin, 2003).
Book, multivolume	[#] H. S. W. Massey, E. H. S. Burhop, and H. B. Gilbody, editors, *Electronic and Ionic Phenomena*, 5 vols. (Clarendon Press, Oxford, 1969–74).

Book, edited	[#] P. Boffi, D. Piccinin, M. C. Ubaldi, editors, *Infrared Holography for Optical Communications: Techniques, Materials, and Devices* (Springer-Verlag, New York, 2003).
Chapter in book	[#] W. Riddle and H. Lee, in *Biomedical Uses of Radiation*, edited by W. R. Hendee (Wiley-VCH, Weinheim, Germany, 1999).
Database	[#] National Institutes of Standards and Technology, Physics Laboratory, Physical Reference Base. <http://physics.nist.gov/PhysRefData/contents.html>.

CITATIONS IN ASTROPHYSICS AND ASTRONOMY

Astronomy and astrophysics don't use the AIP/physics citation style or, for that matter, any single format. But most leading journals are fairly similar. They generally use (author-year) citations in the text, followed by an alphabetical reference list. The reference list follows some fairly common rules. It generally

- uses hanging indents
- contains no bold or italics
- uses authors' initials rather than their first names
- joins coauthors' names with an ampersand "&"
- puts the publication date immediately after the authors' name (with no comma between the name and date)
- omits the titles of articles
- includes titles for books and gives publisher information
- abbreviates journal names, often reducing them to a couple of initials
- lists only the first page of an article
- ends references without a period

Because there's no published style manual for astronomy and astrophysics, citation formats vary. I've standardized them, based on the most common forms in the leading journals. Here are some illustrations, based on *Astronomy and Astrophysics* and the *Astrophysical Journal*, with a little tweaking for consistency.

ASTRONOMY AND ASTROPHYSICS REFERENCE LISTS

Journal article	Boldyrev, S. 2002, ApJ, 569, 841
	Collin, S., Boisson, C., Mouchet, M., et al. 2002, A&A, 388, 771
	Ferrarese, L., & Merritt, D. 2001, ApJ, 555, L79

Journal article, several by same authors	Fürst, E., Reich, W., Reich, P., & Reif, K. 1990a, A&AS, 85, 691
	Fürst, E., Reich, W., Reich, P., & Reif, K. 1990b, A&AS, 85, 805
	Kennicutt, R. 1982a, AJ, 87, 255
	Kennicutt, R. 1982b, ApJ, 253, 101
	Yu, Q. 2002, MNRAS, 331, 935
	Yu, Q., & Tremaine, S. 2002, MNRAS, 335, 965

- ▸ Fürst et al. are listed as 1990a and 1990b because they have the same coauthors.
- ▸ Kennicut's 1982 articles are listed as 1982a and 1982b because they have the same author.
- ▸ Yu's articles are both listed as 2002 (without "a" and "b") because they do not have identical authorship.

Journal article, online	Russeil, D. 2003, A&A 397, 133 DOI: 10.1051/0004-6361:20021504

- ▸ *All* astronomy, astrophysics, and physics articles are online and available through standard scientific databases. Adding the document identifier or other search information may help your readers find them more easily.

Preprint	Barth, A. J., Ho, L. C., & Sargent, W. L. W. 2002, ApJ, to appear [astro-ph/0209562]
	Cordes, J. M., & Lazio, T. J. 2002, preprint [astro-ph/0207156]
	Ergma, E., & Sarna, M. J. 2002, A&A, submitted [astro-ph/0203433]

Book, one author	De Young, D. S. 2002, The Physics of Extragalactic Radio Sources (Chicago: University of Chicago Press)
	Krolik, J. H. 1999, Active Galactic Nuclei (Princeton: Princeton University Press)

Book, multiple authors	Schrijver, C. J., & Zwaan, C. 2000, Solar and Stellar Magnetic Activity (Cambridge: Cambridge University Press)

Chapter in edited book	Johnson, H. L. 1968, in Nebulae and Interstellar Matter, ed. B. M. Middlehurst & L. M. Aller (Chicago: University of Chicago Press), 5

Book in a series	Slane, P. O., & Gaensler, B. M., eds., 2002, Neutron Stars in Supernova Remnants (San Francisco: ASP), ASP Conf. Ser. 271

Chapter in a book in a series	Arnaud, K. A. 1996, in Astronomical Data Analysis Software Systems V, ed. G. Jacoby & J. Barnes (San Francisco: ASP), ASP Conf. Ser. 101, 17 Lacey, C. K. 2002, in Neutron Stars in Supernova Remnants, ed. Patrick O. Slane & Bryan M. Gaensler (San Francisco: ASP), ASP Conf. Ser. 271, 383 Rieger, F. M., & Mannheim, K. 2001, in High Energy Gamma-Ray Astronomy, ed. F. A. Aharonian & H. Völk (Melville, NY: AIP), AIP Conf. Proc. 558, 716

Unpublished paper or dissertation	Egan, M. P., Price, S. D., Moshir, M. M., et al. 1999, Air Force Research Lab. Tech. Rep. no. AFRL-VS. T. R. 1999–1522 Fiore, F., Guainazzi, M., & Grandi, P. 1999, Cookbook for BeppoSAX NFI Spectral Analysis, available by ftp from legacy.gsfc.nasa.gov/sax/doc/software_docs/saxabc _v1.2.ps Kranich, D. 2001, Ph.D. Diss., Technische Universität München

Internet	Skyview, the Internet Virtual Telescope ‹http:// skyview.gsfc.nasa.gov›

Researchers in the physical sciences often cite unpublished research, usually conference papers or work-in-progress that will be published later. Known as preprints (or e-prints), these papers are at the cutting edge of the field and are collected in electronic document archives. Besides collections at major research institutions, there's a huge collection at arXiv.org (http://www.arxiv.org), with mirror sites around the world. Papers are readily accessible and easy to download. What's hard—unless you are on the cutting edge of physics—is actually understanding their content!

Preprints in the arXiv collection are classified by field (physics, astro-physics, mathematics, quantitative biology, and so forth) and, within each field, by major subfields. Papers are submitted to the subfield archives and are numbered by their date of arrival. As with journal articles, the titles of preprints are omitted from citations. Here are some examples:

> Leinson, L. B., Pérez A. 2003, preprint, nucl-th/0312001 <http://www.arxiv.org/PS_cache/nucl-th/pdf/0312/0312001.pdf>
> Watson, A. A. 2003, preprint, astro-ph/0312475
> or
> Watson, A. A. 2003, preprint (astro-ph/0312475)

The classification system is as simple as the papers are complex. Take the Watson paper. It's in astronomy and astrophysics (astro-ph), was submitted in 2003 (03), in the 12th month (12), and was the 475th paper submitted in its category that month (475). Hence, astro-ph/0312475.

For the Leinson article, I included the full URL, but that's not essential. Professionals in the field know where to find arXiv preprints, either at the main archive or mirror sites. It's sufficient to list the ID: nucl-th/0312001.

Preprints like these should be cited and included in your reference list, just like journal articles. Unpublished does not mean uncited.

11 MATHEMATICS AND COMPUTER SCIENCE CITATIONS

Papers in mathematics and computer science use one of two citation styles. The first places an alphabetical reference list at the end of the paper. References in the text are given by bracketed numbers. The first reference might be [23], referring to the twenty-third item in the alphabetical list. The last reference in the article might be [2]. Specific pages are rarely mentioned, but if you need to, use this form: [23, p. 14]. Please use the set of positive integers.

A second system, based on the *Bulletin of the American Mathematical Society*, is often used by advanced mathematicians for publishable research. It, too, has an alphabetical reference list (a slightly different one), but what's unusual are the text references. Instead of bracketed numbers, this style uses abbreviations, based on the author's last name and date of publication. So an article by Hofbauer and Sandholm, published in *Econometrica*, volume 70 (2002), would be cited in the text as something like [HoSa02] or perhaps [HS02] or maybe just [HS]. It's your choice. This abbreviation also appears in the reference list, identifying the entry for Hofbauer and Sandholm's article. In the second table below, I show how to use this AMS *Bulletin* system.

Most books and articles are classified by subfield and uniquely identified in the Mathematical Reviews (MR) Database. Whichever citation system you use, you can include this MR number as the last item in each reference, after the date or page numbers. The MR Database is searchable through the American Mathematical Society's Web site at http://www.ams.org/mrdatabase.

If the article you are citing is available online, perhaps at the author's Web site, mention the URL just before the MR number. If there is no MR number, the Web page appears last.

In the following tables, I show standard mathematical citation forms. Many math journals don't stick to one format. Some use numerical citations for one article and AMS *Bulletin* style for the next. To add to the fun, they'll use the same style differently in different articles. One might list the author as R. Zimmer. The very next article (using the same style) lists the author as Zimmer, R. If I kept looking, I'd probably find one that calls him Bob Zimmer. One article puts the publication date in parentheses; the next one doesn't. In one, the reference list uses italics for every article title and regular type for journal names. The next one does exactly the opposite. Some use boldface for journal numbers, and others don't. Frankly, I don't think any of this matters very much, as long as you are consistent and your professor or publisher is okay with it.

In the tables below, I've swept away these variations and idiosyncrasies. The tables use consistent rules, based on recent editions of major journals in mathematics and computer science.

Article titles and book chapters are italicized. Capitalize only the first word, the first word after a colon, and all proper nouns:

A. R. Conn and P. L. Toint, *An algorithm using quadratic interpolation for unconstrained derivative free optimization*

Book titles are capitalized normally and italicized:

Nonlinear Optimization and Applications

Journal titles are abbreviated but not italicized:

Ann. of Math.
Bull. Amer. Math. Soc.
Geom. Topol.
Trans. Amer. Math. Soc.

A full list of journal abbreviations, compiled by the American Mathematical Society, is available at http://www.ams.org/msnhtml/serials.pdf.

Publications by the same author are listed in the order of publication, beginning with the earliest. Use three em dashes to repeat an author's name, but do so only if *all* the authors are the same. For example:

[32] S. Kihara, *On an elliptic curve over Q(t) of rank* $\geq$ *14*, Proc. Japan Acad. Ser. A Math. Science. 77 (2001), pp. 50–51 MR 2002a:11057.

[33] ———, *On an infinite family of elliptic curves with rank* $\geq$ *14 over Q*, Proc. Japan Acad. Ser. A Math. Science. 73 (1997), p. 32 MR 98d:11059.

[34] S. Kihara and M. Kenku, *Elliptic Curves...*

MATHEMATICS: NUMBERED REFERENCE LIST (ALPHABETICAL ORDER)

Journal article

[1] J. Burkardt, M. Gunzburger, and J. Peterson, *Insensitive functionals, inconsistent gradients, spurious minima, and regularized functionals in flow optimization problems*, Int. J. Comput. Fluid Dyn. 16 (2002), pp. 171–185.

[2] I. D. Coope and C. J. Price, *Positive bases in numerical optimization*, Comput. Optim. Appl. 21 (2003), pp. 169–175.

[3] N. P. Strickland, *Finite subgroups of formal groups*, J. Pure Appl. Algebra 121 (1997), pp. 161–208.

[4] ——, *Gross-Hopkins duality*, Topology 39 (2000), pp. 1021–1033.

▸ Bracketed numbers go in the left margin. Articles are listed in alphabetical order, by author's name.

▸ If an author's name is repeated (and there are no new coauthors), then use three em dashes, followed by a comma. (Em dashes are simply long dashes, about the length of the letter "m." If for some reason, you can't find these em dashes, just use three hyphens.)

Journal article, online

[#] M. Haiman, *Hilbert schemes, polygraphs, and the Macdonald positivity conjecture*, J. Amer. Math. Soc. 14 (2001), pp. 941–1006. Available at http://www.math.berkeley.edu/~mhaiman. MR 2002c:14008.

[#] J. Holt, *Multiple bumping of components of deformation spaces of hyperbolic 3-manifolds*, Amer. J. Math. 125 (2003), pp. 691–736. Available at http://muse.jhu.edu/journals/american_journal_of_mathematics/v125/125.4holt.pdf.

Preprint

[#] J. S. Ellenberg, *Serre's conjecture over F_9*, preprint (2002), submitted for publication. Available at http://www.math.princeton.edu/~ellenber/papers.html.

Preprint (*continued*)	[#] J. Haglund, *Conjectured statistics for the q,* *t-Catalan numbers*, preprint (2003), to appear in Advances in Math. Available at http://www.math.upenn.edu/~jhaglund. [#] R. Miatello and R. Podesta, *The spectrum of* *twisted Dirac operators on compact flat* *manifolds*, preprint (2003). Available at arXiv, math. DG/0312004.

> ▸ In mathematics, as in physics, there's a large, easily
> accessible electronic archive of preprints available
> arXiv. The math collection is at http://www.arxiv
> .org/archive/math. You can cite either the entire
> URL for a preprint, as the reference below for L. W.
> Tu does, or you can simply list the archival number
> and say it is available at arXiv, as the reference for
> Miatello and Podesta does.

	[#] X. Sun, *Singular structure of harmonic maps to* *trees*, preprint (2001), published as *Regularity of* *harmonic maps to trees*, Amer. J. Math. 125 (2003), pp. 737–771. [#] R. Taylor, *On the meromorphic continuation of* *degree two L-functions*, preprint (2003). Available at http://abel.math.harvard .edu/~rtaylor/. [#] L. W. Tu, *A generalized Vandermonde determi-* *nant*, preprint (2003). Available at http://www .arxiv.org/PS_cache/math/pdf/0312/0312446.pdf.

Other unpublished papers	[#] J. S. Ellenberg, *Hilbert modular forms and the* *Galois representations associated to* *Hilbert-Blumenthal abelian varieties*, Ph.D. diss., Harvard University, 1998. [#] P. Hovland, *Automatic differentiation and its role* *in simulation-based optimization*, IMA Workshop, Minneapolis, MN, 2003. [#] M. J. D. Powell, *On the Lagrange functions of* *quadratic models that are defined by* *interpolation*, Tech. Rep. DAMTP 2000/NA10,

Department of Applied Mathematics and
Theoretical Physics, University of Cambridge,
Cambridge, UK, 2000.

Book, one author	[#] S. Alinhac, *Blowup for Nonlinear Hyperbolic Equations, Progr. Nonlinear Differential Equations Appl.*, Vol. 17, Birkhäuser, Boston, 1995. [#] A. Weil, *Basic Number Theory*, Springer-Verlag, Berlin, 1995.
Book, multiple authors	[#] P. E. Gill, W. Murray, and M. H. Wright, *Practical Optimization*, Academic Press, London, 1981. ▸ If there are many authors, then name only the first and add "et al." Example: P. E. Gill et al., *Practical Optimization*...
Book, multiple editions	[#] R. Fourer, D. M. Gay, and B. W. Kernighan, *AMPL: A Modeling Language for Mathematical Programming*, 2nd ed., Thomson/Brooks/Cole, Pacific Grove, CA, 2003.
Book, multivolume	[#] R. Fletcher, *Practical Methods of Optimization*, 2nd ed., Vol. 2, Wiley and Sons, New York, 1980. [#] M. Reed and B. Simon, *Methods of Modern Mathematical Physics* I. *Functional Analysis*, Academic Press, New York, 1980. [#] G. W. Stewart, *Matrix Algorithms. Volume I: Basic Decompositions*, SIAM, Philadelphia, 1998.
Book, edited	[#] F. E. Browder (ed.), *Proc. Symposia in Pure Math.*, vol. 18, part 2, *Nonlinear Operators and Nonlinear Equations of Evolution in Banach Spaces*, Amer. Math. Soc., Providence, 1976. [#] U. Hornung (ed.), *Homogenization and Porous Media*, Springer, Berlin, 1996.

Chapter in edited book	[#] A. R. Conn and P. L. Toint, *An algorithm using quadratic interpolation for unconstrained derivative free optimization*, in *Nonlinear Optimization and Applications*, G. Di Pillo and F. Giannessi, eds., Kluwer Academic/Plenum Publishers, New York, 1996, pp. 27–47. ▸ Notice that the chapter is capitalized like a sentence, but the book title is capitalized normally.
Chapter in multivolume edited book	[#] W. E. Hart, *A stationary point convergence theory of evolutionary algorithms*, in *Foundations of Genetic Algorithms 4*, R. K. Belew and M. D. Vose, eds., Morgan Kaufmann, San Francisco, 1997, pp. 127–134.
Software	[#] T. G. Kolda, P. D. Hough, G. Gay, S. Brown, D. Dunlavy, and H. A. Patrick, *APPSPACK (Asynchronous parallel pattern search package)*; software available at http://software.sandia.gov/appspack. [#] *MultiSimplex 2.0*. Grabitech Solutions AB, Sundvall, Sweden, 2000; software available at http://www.multisimplex.com. ▸ When there is no author, as with this software program, alphabetize by its title.

Now, let's turn to the AMS *Bulletin* style. A few general points:

- To repeat an author's name, use three em dashes instead of the name. But do so only if *all* authors are the same.
- Capitalize only the first word (and proper nouns) for *article* titles. For book and journal titles, on the other hand, capitalize all important words; journal titles are also abbreviated.
- When the place of publication is contained in the publisher's name and is well known, then omit the place-name. Examples: Oxford UP, Cambridge UP, Princeton UP, and U Chicago P.

- To differentiate publications by the same author, include numbers after the initials. For example, assume you are citing one article published by J. Holt in 2002 and another in 2004. You could label them as [Ho2] and [Ho4], or as [Ho02] and [Ho04].
- To denote unpublished articles, you may add an asterisk if you wish, such as [Hop98*], but that is optional.

It may be helpful to see these AMS *Bulletin* citations used in an article text. Here are a couple of examples:

This question was posed by Pyber [Py3] and answered by Murray [Mu].
In [Bo98], uniform barriers are handled differently.

MATHEMATICS: AMS *BULLETIN* STYLE (ALPHABETICAL ORDER)

Journal article	[ATW02]	A.B. Ania, T. Tröger and A. Wambach: *An evolutionary analysis of insurance markets with adverse selection*, Games Econ. Behav. **40** (2002), 153–184.
		▸ Initials such as A.B. have no spaces between them.
		▸ Articles and chapters are capitalized in sentence style. Titles of books and journals, on the other hand, are capitalized normally. Journal titles are abbreviated.
		▸ Volume or issue numbers are boldface.
	[Bo91]	I.M. Bomze: *Cross entropy minimization in uninvadable states of complex populations*, J. Math. Biol. 30 (1991), 73–87. MR **92j**:92012
		▸ There is no punctuation after the MR number.
Journal article, online	[Ha01]	M. Haiman: *Hilbert schemes, polygraphs, and the Macdonald positivity conjecture*, J. Amer. Math. Soc. **14** (2001), 941–1006. Available at http://www.math.berkeley.edu/~mhaiman. MR **2002c**:14008

Journal article, online (*continued*)	[Ho03]	J. Holt: *Multiple bumping of components of deformation spaces of hyperbolic 3-manifolds*, Amer. J. Math. **125** (2003), 691–736. Available at http://muse.jhu.edu/journals/american_journal_of _mathematics/v125/125.4holt.pdf.
Preprint	[BEV]	A. Bravo, S. Encinas and O. Villamayor: *A simplified proof of desingularization and applications*, preprint (2002). Available at http://arXiv.org/abs/math/0206244.
Other unpublished papers	[Hop96]	M. J. Hopkins: *Course note for elliptic cohomology*, unpublished notes (1996).
	[Hop98]	——: *K(1)-local E_∞ ring spectra*, unpublished notes (1998).
	[Mu]	S. Murray: *Conjugacy classes in maximal parabolic subgroups of the general linear group.* Ph.D. diss. (1999), University of Chicago.
Book, individual author	[Cr03]	R. Cressman: *Evolutionary Dynamics and Extensive Form Games.* MIT Press, Cambridge, MA, 2003. ▸ If you are citing several works by Cressman, you could name them by their year of publication, such as [Cr98], [Cr02]; or you could name them [Cr1], [Cr2].
Book, multiple authors	[HaSe88]	J.C. Harsany and R. Selten: *A General Theory of Equilibrium Selection in Games.* MIT Press, Cambridge, MA, 1988. MR **89j**: 90285
Book, multiple editions	[vD91]	E. van Damme: *Stability and Perfection of Nash Equilibria*, 2nd ed., Springer, Berlin, 1991. MR **95f**:90001

Book, multivolume	[Rot]	E. E. Rothman: *Reducing Round-off Error in Chebyshev Pseudospectral Computations.* In: M. Durand and F. El Dabaghi (eds.), *High Performance Computing II.* Elsevier/North-Holland, Amsterdam, 1991, pp. 423–439.
Chapter in multivolume book	[Py3]	L. Pyber: *Group enumeration and where it leads us*, in *European Congress of Mathematics: Budapest July 22–26, 1996*, vol. 2. Birkhäuser, Basel, 1998. MR **99i**:20037
Book, edited	[DR98]	L.A. Dugatkin and H.K. Reeve (eds.): *Game Theory and Animal Behaviour.* Oxford UP, 1998.
	[Na02]	J. Nash: *The Essential John Nash*, H.W. Kuhn and S. Nasar (eds.), Princeton UP, 2002. MR **2002k**:01044
Chapter in edited book	[Bo98]	I.M. Bomze: *Uniform barriers and evolutionarily stable sets.* In: W. Leinfellner, E. Köhler (eds.), *Game Theory, Experience, Rationality.* Kluwer, Dordrecht, 1998, pp. 225–244. MR **2001h**:91020
Book, online	[PU1]	F. Przytycki and M. Urbański: *Fractals in the Plane—The Ergodic Theory Methods.* Available at http://www.math.unt.edu/ ~urbanski, to appear in Cambridge UP.

▸ Some authors add an asterisk to denote unpublished articles, for example: [PU1*]. The number 1 indicates that there are other cited books by the same coauthors, such as PU2.

TEXT STYLE IN MATHEMATICS

Finally, all math papers (regardless of their citation format) have special rules governing the way to present standard terms such as theorems and proofs, as well as the way to present the text following these terms.

Mathematical Term	Proper Format for this Term			Text after the Term
THEOREM	THEOREM	or	**Theorem**	*Italicized*
LEMMA	LEMMA	or	**Lemma**	*Italicized*
COROLLARY	COROLLARY	or	**Corollary**	*Italicized*
PROOF	*Proof*			Standard, no italics
DEFINITION	*Definition*			Standard, no italics
NOTE	*Note*			Standard, no italics
REMARK	*Remark*			Standard, no italics
OBSERVATION	*Observation*			Standard, no italics
EXAMPLE	*Example*			Standard, no italics

For more details, see Ellen Swanson, *Mathematics into Type*, updated by Arlene O'Sean and Antoinette Schleyer (Providence, RI: American Mathematical Society, 1999). *The Chicago Manual of Style*, chapter 14, provides an alternative guide to formatting. Either is fine as long as you are consistent.

12 *BLUEBOOK* LEGAL CITATIONS

Legal citations are commonly based on *The Bluebook: A Uniform System of Citation*, published by the Harvard Law Review.[1] Recently, the Association of Legal Writing Directors developed an alternative manual for classroom use, *The ALWD Citation Manual*.[2] The two systems are similar but not identical, so I will cover them in separate chapters.

Despite its simple and inviting name, the *Bluebook* is actually a detailed reference manual, and often a complicated one. Traditions of legal writing and referencing add to the complexity. A commonplace task like citing an article is a good example of this complexity. Using standard *Bluebook* style, you need to use three different typefaces: ordinary Roman, *italics*, and SMALL CAPS. Take this article, which appears in volume 40 of the *Virginia Journal of International Law*, beginning on page 1103:

> Anne-Marie Slaughter, *Judicial Globalization*, 40 VA. J. INT'L L. 1103 (2000).

Not every legal journal follows these conventions, but many do and no other style is so widely used.[3] In the table of citations below, I'll concentrate on this standard version.

Notice, too, that legal citations frequently use abbreviations. In fact, the *Bluebook* has page after page listing abbreviations for journals, courts,

---

1. *The Bluebook: A Uniform System of Citation*, 18th ed. (Cambridge, MA: Harvard Law Review Association, 2005). By the way, the *Bluebook*'s citation for itself is

THE BLUEBOOK: A UNIFORM SYSTEM OF CITATION (Harvard Law Review Ass'n et al. eds., 18th ed. 2005).

2. Association of Legal Writing Directors and Darby Dickerson, *The ALWD Citation Manual: A Professional System of Citation*, 2d ed. (New York: Aspen Publishers, 2003). I cover this style in chapter 13.

3. Although the *Bluebook* is standard, many law reviews vary from it. There's nothing wrong with these variations, but we'll stick to the *Bluebook* style here to keep things as clear as possible.

legislative documents, and so on. There is no single online site with all these abbreviations, but some sites go part of the distance. The University of Washington Law Library has a helpful list of journal abbreviations at http://lib.law.washington.edu/cilp/abbrev.html. I have added a short list of abbreviations for other common legal terms at the end of this chapter.

Amid this complexity, there is at least one shortcut. You don't need to construct a bibliography. The first footnote gives complete information about the item.

INDEX OF *BLUEBOOK* CITATIONS IN THIS CHAPTER

LEGAL CITATIONS: *BLUEBOOK* STYLE

Journal article

Eric A. Posner & Adrian Vermeule, *Interring the Nondelegation Doctrine*, 69 U. CHI. L. REV. 1721 (2002).

▶ Two authors are separated by "&." If there are three or more authors, you can choose between two ways of listing them. One is to list only the first author, followed by "et al." Alternatively, you can list all the authors, separated by commas, except for an ampersand before the last one: Alfred Adams, Ben Brown & Charles Clark.

▶ The small caps used here for the journal title can be found under Format/Font in Microsoft Word.

Eugene Volokh et al., *The Second Amendment as Teaching Tool in Constitutional Law Classes*, 48 J. LEGAL EDUC. 591, 595–98 (1998).

▶ Let's decode this citation for Volokh's article: it appears in volume 48 of the *Journal of Legal Education*, beginning on page 591. Within the article, I am citing pages 595–98. The same pagination format applies to court cases, laws, and other items. First list the document's opening page, then mention the specific pages you are citing.

Later citations

See Posner & Vermeule, *supra* note 99, at 1723.

▶ The *Bluebook* italicizes the term *see* because it is a "signaling term." There are many such terms, including *e.g.*, *cf.*, and *compare.*

▶ "*Supra* note 99" tells the reader that the full reference to Posner and Vermeule is given above at footnote 99. Of course, this could be easily said in English: "cited in note 99." But, alas, legal citations don't permit it.

Id. at 1724–25.

▶ This refers to the same article as the previous note, but different pages.

Journal article, with quotation in footnote

Russell Korobkin, *Bounded Rationality, Standard Form Contracts, and Unconscionability*, 70 U. CHI. L. REV. 1203, 1203 (2003) ("If anything, the dominance of form contracts over negotiated contracts has increased" over the past thirty years.).

▸ Notice that in legal citations quotes within footnotes come after the citation and are placed in parentheses.

Journal article, online	John J. Brogan, *Speak & Space: How the Internet Is Going to Kill the First Amendment as We Know It*, 8 VA.J.L. & TECH. 8 (2003), http://www.vjolt.net/vol8/issue2/v8i2_a08 -Brogan.pdf.

François Brochu, *The Internet's Effect on the Practice of Real Property Law: A North American Perspective*, 2003 (2) J. INFO. L. & TECH., http://www2.warwick.ac.uk/fac/soc/law/ elj/jilt/2003_2/brochu/.

Unpublished paper or thesis	Tim Wu, *Intellectual Property, Innovation, and Decision Architectures* (Univ. of Chicago Pub. Law Working Paper No. 97, June 2005), *available at* http://www.law.uchicago .edu/academics/publiclaw/97-tw-architectures.pdf.

▸ If you know when a forthcoming paper will be published, include the year: (forthcoming 2007).

Gregory M. Heiser, Fictions of Sovereignty: Legal Interpretation and the Limits of Narrative (1998) (unpublished Ph.D. dissertation, Pennsylvania State University), *available at* http://faculty-staff.ou.edu/H/Gregory.M.Heiser-1/ Dissertation.PDF.

▸ For dissertations, the *Bluebook* does not abbreviate the university's name. For other unpublished papers, it does.

Note or comment in journal	Pintip Hompluem Dunn, Note, *How Judges Overrule: Speech Act Theory and the Doctrine of* Stare Decisis, 113 YALE L.J. 493 (2003).

▸ If the legal term *stare decisis* appeared in regular text, it would be italicized. When it appears as part of an italicized text, such as this note title, its typeface is reversed to normal roman. The same is true for court cases, which are italicized in the regular text of an article and reversed in the citation.

Robert H. Sitkoff, Comment, *"Mend the Hold" and* Erie: *Why an Obscure Contracts Doctrine Should Control in Federal Diversity Cases*, 65 U. CHI. L. REV. 1059 (1998).

▶ If this were a book review, it would say "Book Note" instead of "Comment." The terms "Comments," "Notes," and "Book Notes" refer to student authors.

▶ If there were no author listed for this comment, the citation would begin:

Comment, *"Mend the Hold" and* Erie . . .

A.L.R. annotation	W. E. Shipley, Annotation, *Libel and Slander: Privilege Applicable to Judicial Proceedings as Extending to Administrative Proceedings*, 45 A.L.R.2d 1296 (2003).

▶ *American Law Reports* (A.L.R.) comes in several series. The first series is simply designated "A.L.R." The Federal Series is "A.L.R. Fed."

Odor Detectable by Unaided Person as Furnishing Probable Cause for Search Warrant, 106 A.L.R.5th 397 (2003).

▶ For unsigned annotations, begin with the title.

Book, one author	Bruce Ackerman, We the People: Transformations (1998).

▶ Book authors' names are set in small caps, as are book titles.

Kenneth W. Dam, The Rules of the Global Game: A New Look at U.S. International Policymaking 115–25 (2001).

▶ Refers to pages 115–25.

Book, multiple authors	Douglas G. Baird et al., Game Theory and the Law (1994).

▶ According to the *Bluebook*, if there are more than two authors (as there are for this book) and space is a consideration, you should list only the first name followed by "et al." If space permits, then you may list all the authors:

Douglas G. Baird, Robert H. Gertner & Randal C. Picker, Game Theory and the Law (1994).

Book, multiple editions	Richard A. Posner, Economic Analysis of Law (6th ed. 2003).

Book, single volume in a multivolume work	2 RALPH H. FOLSOM, INTERNATIONAL BUSINESS TRANSACTIONS 76–92 (2d ed. 2002). ▸ This refers to volume 2, pages 76–92.
Book, edited	ECONOMIC ANALYSIS OF THE LAW: SELECTED READINGS (Donald A. Wittman ed., 2003).
Chapter in edited book	Michael Sandel, *What Money Can't Buy: The Moral Limits of Markets*, *in* 21 TANNER LECTURES ON HUMAN VALUES 89 (Grethe B. Peterson ed., 2000).
Reprint of earlier edition	WALTER BAGEHOT, THE ENGLISH CONSTITUTION (Paul Smith ed., Cambridge Univ. Press 2001) (1867). OLIVER WENDELL HOLMES, JR., THE COMMON LAW 2–3 (Little, Brown 1984) (1881).
Star editions such as Blackstone	WILLIAM BLACKSTONE, 4 COMMENTARIES *33. ▸ A few very well-known works, such as Blackstone's *Commentaries on the Laws of England*, are given star treatment. You may cite to the pages in the original by placing an asterisk immediately before the page number. This citation is to vol. 4, page 33. A single asterisk appears before multiple pages: *33–35.
Reporters, court cases, and decisions	Marbury v. Madison, 5 U.S. 137 (1803). ▸ In the text itself, case names are italicized. After the first textual reference, they are usually referred to by the name of the first party: *Marbury.* Roe v. Wade, 410 U.S. 113 (1973). Woodson v. North Carolina, 428 U.S. 280, 305 (1976) (opinion of Stewart, J.). United States v. Emerson, 270 F.3d 203, 260 (5th Cir. 2001). ▸ "F.3d" refers to the *Federal Reporter*, Third Series. 63 F.3d 160 (2d Cir. 1995), *cert. denied*, 516 U.S. 1184 (1996).

► In this citation, the Second Circuit's opinion was appealed to the Supreme Court, which declined to hear the case. One rule of legal citations is that if the case was subsequently appealed, enforced, vacated, or otherwise acted upon, you need to show that in your citation.

Marriage of Friedman, 122 Cal. Rptr. 2d 412 (Ct. App.), *review denied*, No. S109408 (Cal. 2002).

► When citing a case with two or more decisions in a single year, include the year only with the last-cited decision in that year.

Hamdi v. Rumsfeld, 124 S. Ct. 2633, 2661 (2004) (Scalia & Stevens, JJ., dissenting).

In re eBay, Inc. Shareholders Litig., Consolidated C.A. No. 19988-NC, 2004 WL 253521, at *2 (Del. Ch. Jan. 23, 2004) (opinion of Chandler, C.).

► This is an electronic citation; "WL" refers to Westlaw. The same format is used for LEXIS.

Brief, transcript, or record	Brief of Petitioners Hamacher & Gratz at 8, Gratz v. Bollinger, 539 U.S. 244 (2003) (No. 02-516).

► You could also cite briefs such as
  Appellant's Opening Brief at 6, Bears v. Packers...
  Respondent's Brief at 4, Ali v. Liston...

Brief of American Psychological Ass'n as Amicus Curiae in Support of Respondents at 12, Grutter v. Bollinger, 539 U.S. 306 (2003) (No. 02-241), *available at* http://www.apa.org/psyclaw/grutter-v-bollinger.pdf.

Transcript of Oral Argument at 21–22, Rumsfeld v. Padilla, 124 S. Ct. 2711(2004) (No. 03-1027), 2004 WL 1066129.

Trial Hearing Record at 2:21, July 24, 2002, Simon v. Navon, 71 F.3d 9 (1st Cir. 1995).

► Typical citation: *Record at 3, Acme v. Road Runner...*

Unpublished judicial opinion	Ecology Works v. Essex Ins., No. 02-15658, 58 Fed. Appx. 714, 2003 U.S. App. LEXIS 4862 (9th Cir. Mar. 17, 2003).

► Some federal opinions are unpublished and do not appear in the *Federal Reporter*. However, unpublished opinions issued by federal appeals courts since January 2001 are available in the privately published *Federal Appendix*. Some are also available on the courts' own Web sites.

Federal rules	Fᴇᴅ. R. Eᴠɪᴅ. 501. ▸ Refers to Federal Rules of Evidence, rule number 501. Fᴇᴅ. R. Cɪᴠ. P. 9. Fᴇᴅ. R. Cʀɪᴍ. P. 32. U.S. Sᴇɴᴛᴇɴᴄɪɴɢ Gᴜɪᴅᴇʟɪɴᴇs Mᴀɴᴜᴀʟ § 2T1.1(b)(2) (1997).
Codification and restatement	Rᴇsᴛᴀᴛᴇᴍᴇɴᴛ (Sᴇᴄᴏɴᴅ) ᴏꜰ Cᴏɴꜰʟɪᴄᴛ ᴏꜰ Lᴀᴡs § 82 (1971). Rᴇsᴛᴀᴛᴇᴍᴇɴᴛ (Tʜɪʀᴅ) ᴏꜰ ᴛʜᴇ Fᴏʀᴇɪɢɴ Rᴇʟᴀᴛɪᴏɴs Lᴀᴡ ᴏꜰ ᴛʜᴇ Uɴɪᴛᴇᴅ Sᴛᴀᴛᴇs §§ 401–404 (1987). ▸ § means section; §§ is the plural.
Federal laws, statutes, Constitution	U.S. Cᴏɴsᴛ. art. I, § 8, cl. 3. ▸ Refers to the U.S. Constitution, article 1, section 8, clause 3. U.S. Cᴏɴsᴛ. amend. V ("No person shall be held to answer for a capital, or otherwise infamous crime … "). Homeland Security Act of 2002, Pub. L. No. 107-296, §§ 223, 312, 871, 116 Stat. 2135, 2156, 2176, 2243 (2002). Telecommunications Act of 1996, Pub. L. No. 104-104, 110 Stat. 56 (1996). Securities Exchange Act of 1934 § 23(a)(1), 15 U.S.C. § 78w (2000). North American Free Trade Implementation Act, Pub. L. No. 103-182, 107 Stat. 2057 (codified at 19 U.S.C. § 3301 (1993)). ▸ Use normal typeface for the titles of laws, statutes, and regulations. Use sᴍᴀʟʟ ᴄᴀᴘs for the title of the Constitution.
Federal code, official and unofficial	42 U.S.C. § 2000e-2(a)(2). Freedom of Information Act, 5 U.S.C. § 552 (1966), *amended by* Pub. L. No. 104-231, 110 Stat. 3048 (1996). 42 U.S.C. § 2000e-2(a)(2) (2000). ▸ United States Code (U.S.C.) is the official consolidation and codification of U.S. law. Unofficial versions are published by West and LEXIS. The one from West (and Westlaw) is called U.S. Code Annotated (U.S.C.A.). The one from LEXIS is U.S. Code Service (U.S.C.S.). 18 U.S.C.A. § 3553(a) (West 2000 & Supp. 2004).

Regulations and agency materials	Implementation of the Local Competition Provisions in the Telecommunications Act of 1996, 61 Fed. Reg. 45,476, 45,493 (Aug. 29, 1996).
	Promoting Wholesale Competition Through Open Access Non-discriminatory Transmission Services by Public Utilities; Recovery of Stranded Costs by Public Utilities and Transmitting Utilities, 75 Fed. Energy Reg. Comm'n Rep. (CCH) ¶ 61,080, Fed. Energy Reg. Comm'n Rep.—Stat. & Reg. (CCH) ¶ 31,036, 61 Fed. Reg. 21,540 (May 10, 1996).
	Appropriate Framework for Broadband Access to the Internet over Wireline Facilities, 67 Fed. Reg. 9232 (proposed Feb. 28, 2002).

State and local laws, codes	CAL. HEALTH & SAFETY CODE § 11488.4(i)(3) (West 2001).
	CAL. PENAL CODE § 667(b)–(i), *amended by* 1994 Cal. Stat. ch. 12, § 1 (legislative version effective Mar. 8, 2000).
	ILL. CONST. of 1970, art. 5, § 12 (expressly conferring upon the governor the power to reprieve death sentences).
	Washington State Medical Use of Marijuana Act, WASH. REV. CODE ch. 69.51A, 1999 c 2 (Initiative Measure No. 692, approved Nov. 3, 1998).

State court decisions	People v. Latona, 184 Ill. 2d 260, 277 (1998).
	Commonwealth v. Lockwood, 109 Mass. 323, 336 (1872).

Treaty	Agreement Between the United States and Japan Concerning the Treaty of Mutual Cooperation and Security, Jan. 19, 1960, 11 U.S.T. 3420, 131 U.N.T.S. 83 (entered into force June 23, 1960).
	Protocol [No. 1] to the Convention for the Protection of Human Rights and Fundamental Freedoms, Mar. 20, 1952, E.T.S. No. 9, 213 U.N.T.S. 262 [hereinafter European Convention on Human Rights].
	▸ Since there is no obvious way to shorten this lengthy title, the "hereinafter" phrase tells the reader how you will shorten it for use in later citations. A subsequent reference would read:
	European Convention on Human Rights, *supra* note 132.
	CONSOLIDATED TREATY ON EUROPEAN UNION, Oct. 2, 1997, 1997 O.J. (C 340) 145.

Treaty (*continued*)	▶ Because this treaty effectively forms the EU constitution, its title is in small caps, as a constitution would be. North American Free Trade Agreement (NAFTA), Dec. 17, 1992, 32 I.L.M. 605 (1993). ▶ I.L.M. = International Legal Materials
Arbitration	NASD Code Arb. Proc. 10332. ICC R. Arb. art. 8(2). Wheatland Farms, Inc. v. Bakery, Confectionary and Tobacco Workers Local 111, 102 Lab. Arb. Rep. (BNA) 1175 (1994) (Woolf, Arb.).
Patent	U.S. Patent No. 3,819,921 (filed Dec. 21, 1972). ▶ Or if you wish to include the patent's name: Miniature Electronic Calculator, U.S. Patent 3,819,921 (filed Dec. 21, 1972). ▶ You may also include the patent's issuing date, if that is relevant: Miniature Electronic Calculator, U.S. Patent 3,819,921 (filed Dec. 21, 1972) (issued June 25, 1974).
Newspaper article	Howard W. French, *China Luring Foreign Scholars to Make Its Universities Great*, N.Y. TIMES, Oct. 28, 2005, at 1. Thom Shanker, *U.S. and Japan Agree to Strengthen Military Ties*, N.Y. TIMES, Oct. 29, 2005, http://www.nytimes.com/2005/10/30/politics/30bases.html?pagewanted=all.
Book review	Stephen Labaton, *Click Here for Democracy*, N.Y. TIMES, May 13, 2001 (reviewing CASS SUNSTEIN, REPUBLIC.COM (2001)), *available at* http://www.nytimes.com/books/01/05/13/reviews/010513.13labatot.html. Michael Sullivan & Daniel J. Solove, *Can Pragmatism Be Radical? Richard Posner and Legal Pragmatism*, 113 YALE L.J. 687 (2003) (book review). Book Note, *Measuring the Costs of Humanitarian Efforts*, 118 HARV. L. REV. 1031 (2005). ▶ Or

Book Note, *Measuring the Costs of Humanitarian Efforts*, 118 HARV. L. REV. 1031 (2005) (reviewing DAVID KENNEDY, THE DARK SIDES OF VIRTUE: REASSESSING INTERNATIONAL HUMANITARIANISM).

▶　Or

Jane Doe, Book Note, *Measuring . . .*

Interview	Telephone Interview with Sandra Day O'Connor, Associate Justice of the Supreme Court (Jan. 30, 2004). ▶　An in-person interview would be Interview with Emilio Garza, Judge of the Fifth Circuit Court of Appeals, in New Orleans, La. (Feb. 2, 2006).
Speech or lecture	Associate Justice Anthony M. Kennedy, Speech at the American Bar Association Annual Meeting (Aug. 9, 2003), *available at* http://www.supremecourtus.gov/publicinfo/speeches/sp_08-09-03.html. President George W. Bush, Statement on the Next Steps in Strategic Partnership with India (Jan. 12, 2004), 40 WEEKLY COMP. PRES. DOC. 61 (Jan. 19, 2004), *available at* http://www.state.gov/p/sa/rls/pr/28109.htm.
Dictionary or reference work	BLACK'S LAW DICTIONARY 778 (8th ed. 2004). *Income*, *in* BLACK'S LAW DICTIONARY 778 (8th ed. 2004). 6 MARTINDALE-HUBBELL LAW DIRECTORY LA347B (2005) (listing for Charles L. Stern, Jr.). ▶　Refers to volume 6, page LA347B, referring to lawyers in Louisiana. *Supreme Court of the United States*, *in* 10 WEST'S ENCYCLOPEDIA OF AMERICAN LAW 12–14 (1998). ▶　Refers to volume 10, pages 12–14. ▶　The *Bluebook* does not show citations for dictionary definitions and encyclopedia references. This format is based on *Bluebook* guidelines for similar works.

Database	National Law Center for Inter-American Free Trade, Intellectual Property Treaties, InterAm Database, http://natlaw.com/treaties/intpro.htm.

DVD or CD-ROM	PHILLIP B. TAYLOR, CONSTITUTIONAL LAW (PUBLIC LAW) (ICLS Law Lecture Series CD-ROM, n.d.).
	▶ n.d. = no date given for this CD-ROM.

Government document	149 CONG. REC. H2051–53 (daily ed. Mar. 19, 2003).

U.S. Military Commitments and Ongoing Military Operations Abroad: Testimony Before the Senate Armed Services Comm., 108th Cong. 1 (2003) (statement of Paul Wolfowitz, Deputy Defense Secretary), *available at* http://www.senate.gov/~armed_services/statemnt/2003/September/Wolfowitz.pdf.

Human Cloning Prohibition Act of 2001: Hearings on H.R. 1644 Before the Subcomm. on Crime of the House Comm. on the Judiciary, 107th Cong. 51–54 (2001) (statement of Jean Bethke Elshtain), *available at* http://judiciary.house.gov/legacy/72982.pdf.

H.R. REP. NO. 108-507, at 2 (2004), *reprinted in* 2004 U.S.C.C.A.N. 726, 727.

▶ Or

Marine Turtle Conservation Act of 2003, H.R. REP. NO. 108-507, at 2 (2004), *reprinted in* 2004 U.S.C.C.A.N. 726, 727.

THE NATIONAL SECURITY STRATEGY OF THE UNITED STATES OF AMERICA (Sept. 17, 2002), *available at* http://www.whitehouse.gov/nsc/nss.pdf.

U.S. Census Bureau, U.S. Dept. of Commerce, STATISTICAL ABSTRACT OF THE UNITED STATES 15 (123d ed. 2003).

U.S. Census Bureau, U.S. Dept. of Commerce, CENSUS 2000 CONGRESSIONAL DISTRICT SUMMARY FILE DVD (Software Version): 108th Congress (2003).

UN document	U.N. CHARTER art. 23, para. 1.

S.C. Res. 1441, U.N. Doc S/RES/1441 (Nov. 8, 2002).

▶ This is U.N. Security Council Resolution 1441, which found Iraq in "material breach" of previous resolutions.

U.N. Doc. S/PV.4692, at 5 (2003) ("Regrettably, the 12,000 page declaration [by the Iraqi government], most of which is a reprint of earlier documents, does not seem to contain any new evidence that would eliminate the questions or reduce their number.").

Universal Declaration of Human Rights, G.A. Res. 217A, pmbl., U.N. Doc. A/810, at 71 (1948), *available at* http://www .unhchr.ch/udhr/lang/eng.htm.

International courts	Military and Paramilitary Activities In and Against Nicaragua (Nicar. v. U.S.), 1984 I.C.J. 392 (Nov. 26). Prosecutor v. Nikolić, Case IT-94-2-A, Judgment (Feb. 4, 2005), *available at* http://www.un.org/icty/nikolic/appeal/judgement/nik-jsa050204e.pdf.
Foreign court decisions	Jaston & Co. v. McCarthy, [1998] 59 B.C.L.R.3d 168 (Ct. App.). ▸ B.C.L.R.3d = *British Columbia Law Reports*, Third Series Canadian Council of Churches v. The Queen & Others, [1992] 1 S.C.R. 236. ▸ S.C.R. = *Supreme Court Reports* (Canada)
Web site or Web page	U.S. Dep't of State, *What the Secretary Has Been Saying*, 2005, http://www.state.gov/secretary/rm. ▸ You may add the date when the site was last visited: ... secretary/rm/ (last visited Aug. 31, 2005).
E-mail	E-mail from Martha Bergmark, President, Mississippi Center for Justice, to Charles Lipson (Oct. 25, 2005) (on file with author). ▸ You may wish to include the exact time of the message: (Oct. 25, 2005, 9:53 PM CST).

COMMON LEGAL SYMBOLS AND ABBREVIATIONS

affirmed	aff'd	District	Dist.	paragraph	¶ or para.
affirming	aff'g	Document	Doc.	paragraphs	¶¶ or paras.
amendment	amend.	Federal	Fed.	preamble	pmbl.
article	art.	Government	Gov't	Regulation	Reg.
Association	Ass'n	judge;	J.	reversed	rev'd
certiorari	cert.	justice		Rules	R.
Commission	Comm'n	judges;	JJ.	section	§
Company	Co.	justices		sections	§§
Constitution	Const.	judgment	J.	title	tit.
Court	Ct.	Law	L.	versus	v.
Department	Dep't				

Note: Capitalization often depends on context. Contractions such as *aff'd* are *not* followed by a period.

EXPLANATORY PHRASES

In these abbreviations, I have not indicated italics. However, explanatory phrases such as *enforced* or *modified* are almost always italicized. They are called explanatory phrases because they explain the history of judicial decisions. Some, such as *cert. denied* and *rev'd*, are also abbreviated. The *Bluebook* (18th ed.) contains a complete list of abbreviations and explanatory phrases in T.6–16, pages 335–79.

Cornell University Law School provides a valuable interactive list of abbreviations, explanatory phrases, and other legal topics at http://www.law .cornell.edu/citation/topics.htm. Another handy source is the 'Lectric Law Library at http://www.lectlaw.com/def.htm.

LEGAL CITATIONS: ALWD STYLE

Journal article   David A. Sonenshein, *Impeaching the Hearsay Declarant*, 74 Temp. L. Rev. 163, 165–66, 169 (2001).

- ▶ Let's decode this citation. It appears in volume 74 of the *Temple Law Review*, beginning on page 163. Within the article, the specific citation is to pages 165–66 and 169. The same pagination format applies to court cases, laws, and other items. Always list the document's opening page. Then if you are citing some specific pages, list them, too.

Eric A. Posner & Adrian Vermeule, *Interring the Nondelegation Doctrine*, 69 U. Chi. L. Rev. 1721 (2002).

- ▶ Two authors are separated by "&." If there are three or more, you may list the first, followed by "et al." Or you may list all the authors, separated by commas, except for an ampersand before the last author:

Eugene Volokh et al., *The Second Amendment as Teaching Tool in Constitutional Law Classes*, 48 J. Leg. Educ. 591, 595–98 (1998).

- ▶ Or

13 ALWD LEGAL CITATIONS

The Association of Legal Writing Directors (ALWD) has devised a citation system for classroom use as an alternative to the standard *Bluebook* system.[1] This chapter will show you how to use the ALWD system and includes plenty of examples so you can cite cases, laws, regulations, journal articles, books, and more. These citations include both print and electronic sources such as LEXIS and Westlaw, which are widely used for legal research. If you need additional details, you can find them in *The ALWD Citation Manual*.[2]

The ALWD system is similar to the *Bluebook* in many ways. It cites statutes the same way, for example. Neither uses a bibliography because the first citation for each item includes all the information. Still, there are some differences. The most obvious are that ALWD includes the names of book publishers and eliminates the use of SMALL CAPS, which the *Bluebook* uses for some titles and authors.

My conclusion: if you already know how to use one of the legal citation systems, you can easily learn to use the other.

INDEX OF ALWD CITATIONS IN THIS CHAPTER

---

1. *The Bluebook: A Uniform System of Citation*, 18th ed. (Cambridge, MA: Harvard Law Review Association, 2005).

2. Association of Legal Writing Directors and Darby Dickerson, *The ALWD Citation Manual: A Professional System of Citation*, 2d ed. (New York: Aspen Publishers, 2003). A separate version for international sources is forthcoming.

Eugene Volokh, Robert J. Cottrol, Sanford Levinson, L.A. Powe, Jr., & Glenn Harlan, *The Second Amendment as Teaching Tool in Constitutional Law Classes*, 48 J. Leg. Educ. 591, 595–98 (1998).

Craig M. Cooley, Student Author, *Forensic Individualization Sciences and the Capital Jury: Are* Witherspoon *Jurors More Deferential to Suspect Science than Non-*Witherspoon *Jurors?* 28 S. Ill. U. L. J. 273–342 (2004).

- ► ALWD citations typically identify student authors as such. The *Bluebook* accomplishes the same thing by calling the article a "comment" or "note," which is how they are identified in the law journals themselves.

- ► If a student author's name is not listed, begin the citation with the phrase "Student Author."

- ► "Witherspoon" refers to a case. If the case were mentioned in the body of an article, it would be italicized to highlight it and separate it from the surrounding text. Since it appears here in an article title, which is itself italicized, the process is reversed. The *Witherspoon* case is set off from the surrounding text by *not* italicizing it.

Later citations   *See* Posner & Vermeule, *supra* n. 99, at 1723.

- ► ALWD italicizes the term *see* because it is a "signaling term." There are many such terms, including *e.g.*, *cf.*, and *compare*.

- ► "*Supra* n. 99" tells the reader that the full reference to Posner and Vermeule is given above at footnote 99 and that this reference is to page 1723 in their article. (If the reference to footnote 99 appears in the text rather than in a note, the word "note" is spelled out.)

Id.

- ► Refers to the same article and page as the note immediately preceding it. (In nonlegal texts, the term *ibid.* is used instead.)

Id. at 1724–25.

- ► Refers to the same article as the preceding note but to different pages.

Id. at ¶ 2.
Id. at §§ 23–26.

- ► Refers to the same article as the preceding note but to different paragraphs, sections, or other locators.

Journal article, with quotation in footnote	Russell Korobkin, *Bounded Rationality, Standard Form Contracts, and Unconscionability*, 70 U. Chi. L. Rev. 1203 (2003) ("If anything, the dominance of form contracts over negotiated contracts has increased" over the past thirty years.).

▶ In legal citations, quotes or comments within footnotes come after the citation and are placed in parentheses.

Journal article, online	François Brochu, *The Internet's Effect on the Practice of Real Property Law: A North American Perspective*, 2003 (2) J. Info. L. & Tech., http://www2.warwick.ac.uk/fac/ soc/law/elj/jilt/2003_2/brochu.

John J. Brogan, *Speak & Space: How the Internet Is Going to Kill the First Amendment as We Know It*, 8 Va. J.L. & Tech. 8 (2003), http://www.vjolt.net/vol8/issue2/v8i2 _a08-Brogan.pdf.

▶ Citations may also include the date you accessed an online source:

... http://www.vjolt.net/vol8/issue2/v8i2_a08-Brogan.pdf (accessed Jan. 4, 2005).

Unpublished paper or thesis	Michael Barnett, *The Best of Times, the Worst of Times: The Evolution of the Humanitarianism and the UNHCR* (unpublished ms., Apr. 1, 2004) (on file with Program on International Politics, Economics, and Security, U. of Chicago).

Cass R. Sunstein, *Why Does the American Constitution Lack Social and Economic Guarantees?* (U. of Chicago Pub. L. Working Paper No. 36, 2003) (available at http://papers .ssrn.com/sol3/papers.cfm?abstract_id=375622).

Elizabeth Borgwardt, *An Intellectual History of the Atlantic Charter: Ideas, Institutions, and Human Rights in American Diplomacy, 1941–1946* (unpublished Ph.D. dissertation, Stan. U. 2002) (on file with Stan. Dept. History).

Gregory M. Heiser, *Fictions of Sovereignty: Legal Interpretation and the Limits of Narrative* (unpublished Ph.D. dissertation, Pa. St. U. 1998) (available at http:// faculty-staff.ou.edu/H/Gregory.M.Heiser-1/Dissertation.PDF).

Note, comment, or article by student author in journal	Pintip Hompluem Dunn, Student Author, *How Judges Overrule: Speech Act Theory and the Doctrine of* Stare Decisis, 113 Yale L.J. 493 (2003). ▸ The legal term *stare decisis* is italicized when it appears in regular text. When it appears as part of an italicized text, such as this title, its typeface reverts to normal roman (so that it stands out). The same is true for case names, which are normally italicized but revert to roman typeface when they appear within an italicized title. Robert H. Sitkoff, Student Author, *"Mend the Hold" and* Erie: *Why an Obscure Contracts Doctrine Should Control in Federal Diversity Cases*, 65 U. Chi. L. Rev. 1059 (1998). ▸ If no author were listed, this citation would begin: Student Author, *"Mend the Hold" and* Erie . . .
A.L.R. annotation	W. E. Shipley, *Libel and Slander: Privilege Applicable to Judicial Proceedings as Extending to Administrative Proceedings*, 45 A.L.R.2d 1296 (2003). ▸ American Law Reports (A.L.R.) comes in several series. The first series is simply designated "A.L.R." The Federal Series is "A.L.R. Fed." *Odor Detectable by Unaided Person as Furnishing Probable Cause for Search Warrant*, 106 A.L.R.5th 397 (2003). ▸ For unsigned annotations, begin with the title.
Book, one author	Bruce Ackerman, *We the People: Transformations* (Harv. U. Press 1998). Kenneth W. Dam, *The Rules of the Global Game: A New Look at U.S. International Policymaking* 115–25 (U. Chi. Press 2001). ▸ Refers to pages 115–25. Michel Foucault, *Discipline and Punish: The Birth of the Prison* (Alan Sheridan trans., Pantheon Books 1977).

Book, multiple authors	Douglas G. Baird et al., *Game Theory and the Law* (Harv. U. Press 1994).
	▸ According to ALWD, if there are three or more authors (as there are for this book), you may list only the first name followed by "et al." If you wish to include the other authors' names as well, the citation would be
	Douglas G. Baird, Robert H. Gertner & Randal C. Picker, *Game Theory and the Law* (Harv. U. Press 1994).
Book, single volume in a multivolume work	Ralph H. Folsom et al., *International Business Transactions* vol. 2, 76–92 (2d ed., West Group 2002).
	▸ No comma between the title and volume number.
Book, edited	*Economic Analysis of the Law: Selected Readings* (Donald A. Wittman ed., Blackwell Publishers 2003).
	▸ No comma between the name of the editor and "ed."
	Competition Laws in Conflict: Antitrust Jurisdiction in the Global Economy (Richard A. Epstein & Michael S. Greve eds., AEI Press 2004).
Chapter in edited book	Kenneth W. Abbott & Duncan Snidal, *Hard and Soft Law in International Governance*, in *Legalization and World Politics* 37 (Judith L. Goldstein et al. eds., MIT Press 2001).
Reprint of earlier edition	Walter Bagehot, *The English Constitution* (Paul Smith ed., Cambridge U. Press 2001) (originally published 1867).
	Oliver Wendell Holmes, Jr., *The Common Law* 2–3 (Little, Brown 1984) (originally published 1881).
Star editions such as Blackstone	William Blackstone, *Commentaries* vol. 4, *33.

► A few very well-known works, such as Blackstone's
Commentaries on the Laws of England, are given star
treatment. You may cite to the pages in the original by placing
an asterisk immediately before the page number. This citation
is to volume 4, page 33. A double asterisk appears before
multiple pages: **33–35.

Reporters, court cases, and decisions	*Marbury v. Madison*, 5 U.S. 137 (1803). ► After the first textual reference, cases are usually referred to by the name of the first party: *Marbury*. *Roe v. Wade*, 410 U.S. 113 (1973). *Woodson v. North Carolina*, 428 U.S. 280, 305 (1976) (opinion of Stewart, J.). *Hamdi v. Rumsfeld*, 124 S. Ct. 2633, 2661 (2004) (Scalia & Stevens, JJ., dissenting). *U.S. v. Emerson*, 270 F.3d 203, 260 (5th Cir. 2001). ► Case names are italicized in text and footnotes. "F.3d" refers to the *Federal Reporter*, Third Series. 63 F.3d 160 (2d Cir. 1995), *cert. denied*, 516 U.S. 1184 (1996). ► One rule of legal citations is that if the case was subsequently appealed, enforced, vacated, or otherwise acted upon, you need to show that in your citation. In this citation, the Second Circuit's opinion was appealed to the Supreme Court, which declined to hear the case. The citation should include the year for each decision. *Marriage of Friedman*, 122 Cal. Rptr. 2d 412 (Ct. App. 2002), *review denied*, No. S109408 (Cal. 2002). *In re eBay, Inc. Shareholders Litig.*, Consolidated C.A. No. 19988-NC, 2004 WL 253521 (Del. Ch. Jan. 23, 2004) (opinion of Chandler, Chan.). ► This is an electronic citation; "WL" refers to Westlaw. The same format is used for LEXIS.

Brief, transcript, or record	Br. Petrs. Hamacher & Gratz at 8, *Gratz v. Bollinger*, 539 U.S. 244 (2003). ► This refers to the Brief of Petitioners Hamacher and Gratz for the Supreme Court case of *Gratz v. Bollinger*.

Amicus Curiae Br. American Psychological Assn. in Support of Respts. at 12, *Grutter v. Bollinger*, 539 U.S. 306 (2003) (available at http://www.apa.org/psyclaw/ grutter-v-bollinger.pdf).

Oral Argument Transcr. at 21–22, *Rumsfeld v. Padilla*, 124 S. Ct. 2711 (2004) (available at 2004 WL 1066129).

Tr. Hrg. Rec. at 2:21, July 24, 2002, *Simon v. Navon*, 71 F.3d 9 (1st Cir. 1995).

► A typical appellate citation is R. at 3, *Holmes v. Moriarty...*

Unpublished judicial opinion	*Ecology Works v. Essex Ins.*, No. 02-15658, 58 Fed. Appx. 714, 2003 U.S. App. LEXIS 4862 (9th Cir. Mar. 17, 2003). ► Some federal opinions are unpublished and do not appear in the official *Federal Reporter*. Since January 2001, however, unpublished opinions issued by federal appeals courts have been available in the privately published *Federal Appendix*. Some are also available on the courts' own Web sites, which can be cited directly. ► If a case is online but has not yet appeared in the *Federal Appendix*, then: *Ecology Works v. Essex Ins.*, 2003 U.S. App. LEXIS 4862 (9th Cir. Mar. 17, 2003). ► If the online source is Westlaw, use the initials "WL."
Federal rules	Fed. R. Evid. 501. ► Refers to Federal Rules of Evidence, rule number 501. Fed. R. Civ. P. 9. Fed. R. Crim. P. 32. *U.S. Sentencing Guidelines Manual* § 2T1.1(b)(2) (1997).
Codification and restatement	*Restatement (Second) of Conflict of Laws* § 82 (1971). *Restatement (Third) of the Foreign Relations Law of the United States* §§ 401–404 (1987). ► § means "section" and §§ is the plural. Similarly, ¶ means "paragraph" and ¶¶ is the plural.
Federal laws, statutes, Constitution	U.S. Const. art. I, § 8, cl. 3. ► Refers to the U.S. Constitution, article 1, section 8, clause 3.

U.S. Const. amend. V ("No person shall be held to answer for a capital, or otherwise infamous crime...") 15 U.S.C. §78w (2000).

Exchange Act of 1934 § 23(a)(1), 15 U.S.C. § 78w (2000).

Homeland Security Act of 2002, Pub. L. No. 107-296, §§ 223, 312, 871, 116 Stat. 2135, 2156, 2176, 2243 (2002).

▸ This is a "parallel citation," showing two (or more) locations where a law can be found. The examples below also use parallel citations.

Agricultural Bioterrorism Protection Act of 2002 § 212, 116 Stat. 594, 647, 7 U.S.C. § 8401 (2002), as amended by *Homeland Security Act of 2002* § 1709(b), 116 Stat. 2135, 2319 (2002).

Telecommunications Act of 1996, Pub. L. No. 104-104, 110 Stat. 56 (1996).

North American Free Trade Implementation Act, Pub. L. No. 103-182, 107 Stat. 2057 (1993) (codified at 19 U.S.C. § 3301).

Federal code, official and unofficial	*Freedom of Information Act*, 5 U.S.C. § 552 (1966) (amended by Pub. L. No. 104-231, 110 Stat. 3048 (1996)).

42 U.S.C. § 2000e-2(a)(2) (2000).

▸ United States Code (U.S.C.) is the official consolidation and codification of U.S. law. Unofficial versions are published by West and LEXIS. The one from West (and Westlaw) is called U.S. Code Annotated (U.S.C.A.). The one from LEXIS is called U.S. Code Service (U.S.C.S.).

18 U.S.C.A. § 3553(a) (West 2000 & Supp. 2004).

Regulations and agency materials	*Implementation of the Local Competition Provisions in the Telecommunications Act of 1996*, 61 Fed. Reg. 45,476, 45,493 (Aug. 29, 1996).

▸ Each day, the *Federal Register* (Fed. Reg.) publishes official notices, regulations, and proposed regulations by federal agencies, as well as Executive Orders and other presidential documents.

41 C.F.R. § 60-250.20 (2004).

▸ "C.F.R." stands for *Code of Federal Regulations.*

Regulations (*continued*)	41 C.F.R. § 60-250.20 (2004) (http://www.dol.gov/ dol/allcfr/Title_41/Part_60-250/41CFR60-250.20.htm).

Promoting Wholesale Competition through Open Access Non-discriminatory Transmission Services by Public Utilities; Recovery of Stranded Costs by Public Utilities and Transmitting Utilities, 75 Fed. Energy Reg. Commn. Rep. (CCH) ¶ 61,080, Fed. Energy Reg. Commn. Rep.—Stat. & Reg. (CCH) ¶ 31,036, 61 Fed. Reg. 21,540 (May 10, 1996).

Appropriate Framework for Broadband Access to the Internet over Wireline Facilities, 67 Fed. Reg. 9232 (proposed Feb. 28, 2002).

State and local laws, codes

Cal. Health & Safety Code § 123462(c) (available at http://caselaw.lp.findlaw.com/cacodes/hsc/123460 -123468.html) ("The state shall not deny or interfere with a woman's fundamental right to choose to bear a child or to choose to obtain an abortion, except as specifically permitted by this article.").

Cal. Penal Code § 667(b)–(i), *amended by* 1994 Cal. Stat. ch. 12, § 1 (legislative version effective Mar. 8, 2000).

Ill. Const. of 1970, art. 5, § 12 (expressly conferring upon the governor the power to reprieve death sentences).

Md. Est. & Trust Code Ann. § 4-101 (2001 & Supp. 2004).

Washington State Medical Use of Marijuana Act, Wash. Rev. Code ch. 69.51A, 1999 c 2 (Initiative Measure No. 692, approved Nov. 3, 1998).

2004 Ill. Laws 307.

2004 Tenn. Pub. Acts ch. 12.

State court decisions

People v. Latona, 184 Ill. 2d 260, 277 (1998).
Commonwealth v. Lockwood, 109 Mass. 323, 336 (1872).

Treaty

Agreement between the United States and Japan concerning the Treaty of Mutual Cooperation and Security (Jan. 19, 1960) (entered into force June 23, 1960), 11 U.S.T. 3420, 131 U.N.T.S. 83.

Protocol [No. 1] to the Convention for the Protection of Human Rights and Fundamental Freedoms, Mar. 20, 1952, E.T.S. No. 9, 213 U.N.T.S. 262 [hereinafter *European Convention on Human Rights*].

▶ Since there is no obvious way to shorten this lengthy title, the "hereinafter" phrase tells the reader how you will shorten it for use in later citations. A subsequent reference would read: *European Convention on Human Rights, supra* n. 132.

Consolidated Treaty on European Union (Oct. 2, 1997), 1997 O.J. (C340) 145.

Treaty of Westphalia, art. 28 (Oct. 24, 1648) (available at http://fletcher.tufts.edu/multi/texts/historical/ westphalia.txt).

North American Free Trade Agreement (NAFTA) (Dec. 17, 1992), 32 I.L.M. 605 (1993).

▶ I.L.M. = International Legal Materials

Arbitration	NASD Code Arb. Proc. 10332. ICC R. Arb. art. 8(2).
Patent	Jack S. Kilby et al., *Miniature Electronic Calculator*, U.S. Patent 3,819,921 (issued June 25, 1974). Louis Pasteur, *Improvements in the Manufacture and Preservation of Beer and in the Treatment of Yeast and Wort, Together with Apparatus for the Same*, U.S. Patent No. 141,072 (issued July 22, 1873). ▶ Or U.S. Patent No. 141,072 (issued July 22, 1873).
Newspaper article, hard copy and online	Linda Greenhouse, *Supreme Court to Hear Case on Cable as Internet Carrier*, 154 N.Y. Times B4 (Dec. 4, 2004). ▶ Believe it or not, ALWD asks for the volume number of the newspaper; in this case, it is 154. Linda Greenhouse, *Supreme Court to Hear Case on Cable as Internet Carrier*, 154 N.Y. Times B4 (Dec. 4, 2004) (available at http://www.nytimes.com/2004/12/04/business/ 04scotus.html).

Book review	Michael Sullivan & Daniel J. Solove, *Book Review*, 113 Yale L.J. 687 (2003) (reviewing *Can Pragmatism Be Radical? Richard Posner and Legal Pragmatism*).
	Stephen Labaton, *Book Review*, 150 N.Y. Times (May 13, 2001) (reviewing *Republic.com*) (available at http://www.nytimes.com/books/01/05/13/reviews/010513.13labatot.html).
Interview	Telephone Interview with Sandra Day O'Connor, Assoc. J., S. Ct. (Jan. 30, 2004).
	▶ An in-person interview would be Interview with Emilio Garza, J., 5th Cir. (Feb. 2, 2006).
Speech or lecture	Anthony M. Kennedy, Speech (ABA, Aug. 9, 2003) (available at http://www.supremecourtus.gov/publicinfo/speeches/sp_08-09-03.html).
	▶ If the speech had a title, then it would be Anthony M. Kennedy, Speech, *Sentencing Guidelines . . .*
	▶ If a speaker's title or position is not generally known, you should include it: Jonathan F. Fanton, President, John D. and Catherine T. MacArthur Foundation (European Humanities University International, June 9, 2005) (available at http://www.macfound.org/speeches/staff/06_09_2005.htm).
	George W. Bush, Statement, *Next Steps in Strategic Partnership with India* (Jan. 12, 2004), 40 Wkly. Comp. Pres. Docs. 61 (Jan. 19, 2004) (available at http://www.state.gov/p/sa/rls/pr/28109.htm).
Dictionary or reference work	*Black's Law Dictionary* 241 (Bryan A. Garner ed., 8th ed., West 2004).
	68 Am. Jur. 2d *Schools* § 330 (2000 & Supp. 2004).
	▶ Refers to a legal encyclopedia: *American Jurisprudence, Second.* *Martindale-Hubbell Law Directory*, vol. 12, PA53B (Martindale-Hubbell 2004).

▸ Refers to volume 12, page "PA53B."

1A C.J.S. *Accounting* §§ 2–3 (2005).

▸ Refers to *Corpus Juris Secundum.*

Database	Natl. L. Ctr. Inter-Am. Free Trade, Intellectual Property Treaties, InterAm Database, http://natlaw.com/treaties/intpro.htm.
DVD or CD-ROM	Phillip B. Taylor, *Constitutional Law (Public Law)* (ICLS Law Lecture Series, n.d.) (CD-ROM). ▸ n.d. = no date on this CD-ROM. *The Oxford English Dictionary on CD-ROM* (2d ed., Oxford U. Press, version 3.1, 2004).
Government document	149 Cong. Rec. H2051–53 (daily ed. Mar. 19, 2003). *U.S. Military Commitments and Ongoing Military Operations Abroad: Testimony before the Senate Armed Services Comm.*, 108th Cong. 1 (Sept. 9, 2003) (statement of Paul Wolfowitz, Deputy Defense Secretary) (available at http://www.senate.gov/~armed_services/statemnt/2003/September/Wolfowitz.pdf). *Human Cloning Prohibition Act of 2001: Hearings on H.R. 1644 Before the Subcomm. on Crime of the House Comm. on the Judiciary*, 107th Cong. 51–54 (2001) (statement of Jean Bethke Elshtain) (available at http://judiciary.hous.gov/legacy/72982.pdf). H.R. Conf. Rpt. 104-458, at 201 (Jan. 31, 1996). S. Rpt. 108-102, at 16 (July 16, 2003) (reprinted in 2004 U.S.C.C.A.N. 2348, 2360–61). *The National Security Strategy of the United States of America* (Sept. 17, 2002) (available at http://www.whitehouse.gov/nsc/nss.pdf). U.S. Census Bureau, U.S. Dept. of Commerce, *Statistical Abstract of the United States 15* (123d ed. 2003) [hereinafter *2003 Statistical Abstract*]. U.S. Census Bureau, U.S. Dept. of Commerce, *Census 2000 Congressional District Summary File DVD*, 108th Cong. (2003).

UN document	U.N. Charter art. 23, para. 1.
	S.C. Res. 1441, U.N. Doc S/RES/1441 (2002).
	▶ This is U.N. Security Council Resolution 1441, which found Iraq in "material breach" of previous resolutions.
	UN Doc. S/PV.4692, at 5 (2003) ("Regrettably, the 12,000 page declaration [by the Iraqi government], most of which is a reprint of earlier documents, does not seem to contain any new evidence that would eliminate the questions or reduce their number.").
	Universal Declaration of Human Rights, G.A. Res. 217A, pmbl., U.N. Doc. A/810 (1984), at 71 (1948) (available at http://www.unhchr.ch/udhr/lang/eng.htm).
International courts	*Military and Paramilitary Activities In and Against Nicaragua (Nicaragua v. U.S.)*, 1984 I.C.J. 392 (1984).
	Prosecutor v. Nikolić, Case IT-94-2-A (U.N. ICT (App) (Yug) 2005) (Judgment) (available at http://www.un.org/icty/nikolic/appeal/judgement/nik-jsa050204e.pdf).
Foreign court decisions	*Jaston & Co. v. McCarthy*, 59 B.C.L.R.3d 168 (B.C.C.A.) (1998).
	▶ B.C.L.R.3d = *British Columbia Law Reports*, Third Series
	▶ B.C.C.A. = British Columbia Court of Appeal (Canada)
	Canadian Council of Churches v. The Queen & Others, 1 S.C.R. 236 (1992).
	▶ S.C.R. = *Supreme Court Reports* (Canada)
Web site or Web page	U.S. Dept. of State, *What the Secretary Has Been Saying*, 2005, State Department Web Site, http://www.state.gov/secretary/rm.
	▶ You may wish to add the date of access or date when the site was last updated:
	... secretary/rm/ (accessed Aug. 31, 2005).
	... secretary/rm/ (last updated Aug. 28, 2005).

| E-mail | E-mail from Martha Bergmark, President, Mississippi Center for Justice, to Charles Lipson et al., *Settlement of MCJ Lawsuit Secures Access to Counsel at Juvenile Training Schools* (Jan. 13, 2005) (on file with author). |

COMMON LEGAL SYMBOLS AND ABBREVIATIONS

Admission	Admis.	Government	Govt.
Affidavit	Aff.	Journal	J.
amended	amend.	Judge	J.
Amendment	Amend.	Judges, Justices	JJ.
article	art.	Judgment	Judg.
Association	Assn.	Justice	J.
Brief	Br.	Law	L.
Commission	Commn.	note	n.
Company	Co.	notes	nn.
Constitution	Const.	paragraph	¶ or para.
Court	Ct.	paragraphs	¶ or paras.
Defendant	Def.	Petition	Pet.
Department	Dept.	Petitioner	Petr.
District	Dist.	Petitioners	Petrs.
Document	Doc.	Regulation	Reg.
Evidence	Evid.	Rules	R.
Exhibit	Ex.	section	§ or sec.
Federal	Fed.	sections	§§ or secs.

Note: Capitalization often depends on context. Unlike the *Bluebook*, the ALWD does not use contractions such as *dep't*. It uses conventional abbreviations, such as *Dept.* (It does allow contractions for prior and subsequent history.) A list of general abbreviations is given in the *ALWD Citation Manual*, appendix 3.

ACTIONS AND EXPLANATORY PHRASES TO INCLUDE IN COURT DECISIONS

affirmed	*aff'd*
affirmed on other grounds	*aff'd on other grounds*
appeal denied	*appeal denied*
appeal filed	*appeal filed*
certifying question to	*certifying question to*
certiorari denied	*cert. denied*

certiorari dismissed	*cert. dismissed*
certiorari granted	*cert. granted*
enforced	*enforced*
mandamus denied	*mandamus denied*
modified	*modified*
overruled	*overruled*
petition for certiorari filed	*petition for cert. filed*
reversed	*rev'd*
reversed in part and affirmed in part	*rev'd in part and aff'd in part*
reversed in part on other grounds	*rev'd in part on other grounds*
superseded	*superseded*
vacated	*vacated*
withdrawn	*withdrawn*

14 FAQS ABOUT *ALL* REFERENCE
STYLES

WHAT SHOULD YOU CITE?

Do I need to cite everything I use in the paper?
Pretty much. Cite anything you rely on for data or authoritative opinions.
Cite both quotes and paraphrases. Cite personal communications such as
e-mails, interviews, or conversations with professors if you rely on them
for your paper. If you rely heavily on any single source, make that clear,
either with multiple citations or with somewhat fewer citations plus a clear
statement that you are relying on a particular source for a particular topic.

There is one exception. Don't cite sources for facts that are well-known
to your audience. It's overkill to cite any authorities for the signing of the
Declaration of Independence on July 4, 1776. There will be time enough
to footnote them when you start discussing the politics of the Continental
Congress.

How many citations does a paper have, anyway?
It varies and there is no exact number, but a couple per page is common
in well-researched papers. More is fine. If there are no citations for several
pages in a row, something's probably wrong. Most likely, you just forgot
to include them. You need to go back and fix the problem.

How many different sources should I use?
That depends on how complicated your subject is, how intensively you've
studied it, and how long your paper is. If it is a complex subject or one that
is debated intensely, you'll need to reflect that with multiple sources—some
to present facts, some to cover different sides of the issue. On the other hand,
if it's a short paper on a straightforward topic, you might need only a couple
of sources. If you are unsure, ask what your professor expects for your topic.
While you're talking, you might also ask about the best sources to use.

In any case, don't base longer, more complex papers on two or three
sources, even if they are very good ones. Your paper should be more than
a gloss on others' work (unless it is specifically an analysis of that scholar's

work). It should be an original work that stands on its own. Use a variety of sources and make sure they include a range of opinions on any controversial topic.

You certainly don't need to agree with all sides. You are not made of rubber. But, at least for longer papers and hotly debated topics, you need to show that you have read different views, wrestled with varied ideas, and responded to the most important points.

By the way, your notes can be negative citations, as well as positive. You are welcome to disagree openly with a source, or you can simply say, "For an alternative view, see . . ."

WHAT GOES IN A CITATION?

Can I include discussion or analysis in notes?
Yes, for most styles, *except in the sciences*. Footnotes or endnotes are fine spots to add brief insights that bear on your paper topic but would distract from your narrative if they were included in the text. Just remember you still need to edit these discursive notes, just as you do the rest of your writing. And don't let them become a major focus of your writing effort. The text is the main event.

If you use in-text citations such as (Tarcov 2006) and want to add some explanatory notes, you'll have to add them as a special set of citations. They are usually marked with a superscript number.

If you are writing in the sciences and already using superscripts for the citation-sequence system, you're better off avoiding explanatory notes entirely. If you really need to include one or two, mark them with an asterisk or other symbol. In this system, you cannot use numbered citations for anything except references.

I sometimes use articles from *Time* or *Newsweek*. Should they be cited like journal articles or newspaper articles?
That depends on how long and how significant the articles are. Short pieces in newsweeklies are usually treated like newspaper articles. You can include the author, but you don't have to. Either way, short articles are not usually included in the bibliography. Major articles with author bylines are treated more like journal articles and are included in the bibliography.

Some styles, notably Chicago and *Bluebook* legal references, use shortened citations after the first citation for an item. What's the best way to shorten a title?

There are some standard ways. One is to use only the author's last name: Strunk and White instead of William Strunk Jr. and E. B. White. You also drop the initial article in the title and any other needless words. *The Elements of Style* becomes *Elements of Style*. Drop the edition number and all publishing information, such as the publisher's name. For articles, drop the journal title and volume. So:

Long form	[99]William Strunk Jr. and E. B. White, *The Elements of Style*, 4th ed. (New York: Longman, 2000), 12.
	[100]Stefan Elbe, "HIV/AIDS and the Changing Landscape of War in Africa," *International Security* 27 (Fall 2002): 159–77.
Short form	[199]Strunk and White, *Elements of Style*, 12.
	[200]Elbe, "HIV/AIDS."

The shortened title for Elbe's work might be confusing if your paper dealt mainly with HIV/AIDS and was filled with similar citations. For clarity, you might decide on an alternative short title such as Elbe, "Landscape of War."

If the title has two parts, put on your surgical gloves and remove the colon.

Long form	[99]Robert A. Kaster, *Guardians of Language: The Grammarian and Society in Late Antiquity* (Berkeley: University of California Press, 1988).
	[100]Kenneth Shultz and Barry Weingast, "The Democratic Advantage: Institutional Foundations of Financial Power in International Competition," *International Organization* 57 (Winter 2003): 3–42.
Short form	[199]Kaster, *Guardians of Language*.
	[200]Shultz and Weingast, "Democratic Advantage."

You might need to shorten a title by identifying a few key words. Take Francis Robinson, ed., *Cambridge Illustrated History of the Islamic World*. There is no single right way to shorten this, but the best title is probably: Robinson, *History of Islamic World*. (Note that Robinson is simply listed as the author; his title as editor is dropped.)

In the first full note, you can also tell readers how you will shorten a title. After giving the full title for Senate Banking Committee hearings on terrorist money laundering, for instance, you might say: (subsequently called "2004 Senate hearings").

For legal citations, you would say (hereinafter called "2004 Senate hearings"). To shorten legal citations, you also omit any book or article titles. Give only the author's name and say where the first full note is. For example: *See* Rosenberg, *supra* note 3.

What about citing a work I've found in someone else's notes? Do I need to cite the place where I discovered the work?

This issue comes up all the time because it's one of the most important ways we learn about other works and other ideas. Reading a book by E. L. Jones, for example, you find an interesting citation to Adam Smith. As it turns out, you are more interested in Smith's point than in Jones's commentary, so you decide to cite Smith. That's fine—you can certainly cite Smith—but how should you handle it?

There's a choice. One way is to follow the paper trail from Jones's note to Adam Smith's text, read the relevant part, and simply cite it, with no reference at all to Jones. That's completely legitimate for books like Smith's that are well known in their field. You are likely to come across such works in your normal research, and you don't need to cite Jones as the guide who sent you there. To do that honestly, though, you have to go to Smith and read the relevant parts.

The rule is simple: *Cite only texts you have actually used and would have found in the normal course of your research,* not obscure texts used by someone else or works you know about only secondhand. You don't have to read several hundred pages of Adam Smith. You do have to read the relevant pages in Smith—the ones you cite. Remember the basic principle: *When you say you did the work yourself, you actually did it.*

Alternatively, if you don't have time to read Smith yourself (or if the work is written in a language you cannot read), you can cite the text this way: "Smith, *Wealth of Nations*, 123, as discussed in Jones, *The European Miracle*." Normally, you don't need to cite the page in Jones, but you can if you wish. An in-text citation would look different but accomplish the same thing: (Smith 123, qtd. in Jones).

This alternative is completely honest, too. You are referencing Smith's point but saying you found it in Jones. This follows another equally important principle: *When you rely on someone else's work, you cite it.* In this case, you are relying on Jones, not Smith himself, as your source for Smith's point.

Follow the same rule if Jones leads you to a work that is unusual or obscure *to you*, a work you discovered only because Jones did the detailed research, found it, and told you about it. For example, one of Jones's citations is to a 1668 book by Paul Rycaut, entitled *The Present State of the Ottoman Empire*. I'm not an expert on the Ottoman Empire and certainly would not have discovered that book myself. Frankly, I'd never even heard of it until Jones mentioned it. So I'd cite it as (Rycaut 54, cited in Jones). I can do that without going to the Rycaut book. On the other hand, if I were a student of Ottoman history and Jones had simply reminded me of Rycaut's work, I could cite it directly. To do that honestly, however, I would need to go to the Rycaut volume and read the relevant passage.

Some scholars, unfortunately, sneak around this practice. They don't give credit where credit is due. They simply cite Rycaut, even if they've never heard of him before, or they cite Smith, even if they haven't read the passage. One result (and it really happens!) could be that Jones made a mistake in his citation and the next scholar repeated the error. It's really a twofold blunder: an incorrect footnote and a false assertion that the writer used Smith as a source.

The specific rules here are less important than the basic concepts:

- Cite only texts you found in the normal course of your research and have actually used.
- Cite all your sources openly and honestly.

Follow these and you'll do just fine.

BIBLIOGRAPHY

Do I need to have a bibliography?

Yes, for all styles *except* complete Chicago notes and legal citations. If you use *Bluebook*, ALWD, or full Chicago citations, the first note for each item gives readers complete information, including the title and publisher, so you don't need a bibliography. (You are welcome to include a bibliography if you use Chicago style, but you don't have to, unless your professor requires it.)

All other styles require a bibliography for a simple reason. The notes themselves are too brief to describe the sources fully.

Should my bibliography include the general background reading I did for the paper?

The answer depends on how much you relied on a particular reading and which reference style you use. MLA, APA, and science bibliographies include only the works you have actually cited. Chicago-style bibliographies are more flexible and can include works you haven't cited in a note.

My advice is this: If a work was really useful to you, then check to make sure you have acknowledged that debt somewhere with a citation. After you've cited it once, the work will appear in your bibliography, regardless of which style you use. If a particular background reading wasn't important in your research, don't worry about citing it.

Does the bibliography raise any questions about my work?
Yes, readers will scan your bibliography to see what kinds of sources you used and whether they are the best ones. There are five problems to watch out for:

- Old, out-of-date works
- Bias in the overall bibliography
- Omission of major works in your subject
- Reliance on poor or weak sources
- Excessive reliance on one or two sources

These are not really problems with the bibliography, as such. They are problems with the text that become apparent by looking at the bibliography.

Old sources are great for some purposes but antiquated for others. Many consider Gibbon's *Decline and Fall of the Roman Empire* the greatest historical work ever written. But no one today would use it as a major secondary source on Rome or Byzantium. Too much impressive research has been completed in the two centuries since Gibbon wrote. So, if you were writing about current views of Byzantium or ancient Rome, *Decline and Fall* would be out-of-date. Relying on it would cast a shadow on your research. On the other hand, if you were writing about great historical works, eighteenth-century perspectives, or changing views about Byzantium, using Gibbon would be perfectly appropriate, perhaps essential.

"Old" means different things in different fields. A work published ten or fifteen years ago might be reasonably current in history, literature, and some areas of mathematics, depending on how fast those fields are changing. For a discipline moving at warp speed like genetics, an article might be out-of-date within a year. A paper in molecular genetics filled with citations from 1994 or even 2004 would cast serious doubt on the entire project. Whatever your field, you should rely on the best works and make sure they have not been superseded by newer, better research.

Bias, omission of key works, and overreliance on a few sources reveal other problems.[1] Bias means you have looked at only one side of a multi-faceted issue. Your bibliography might indicate bias if it lists readings on only one side of a contested issue. Omitting an authoritative work not only impoverishes your work; it leaves readers wondering if you studied the topic carefully.

The remedy for all these problems is the same. For longer, more complex papers, at least, you need to read a variety of major works in your subject and indicate that with citations.

However long (or short!) your paper, make sure your sources are considered solid and reliable. Your professors and teaching assistants can really help here. They know the literature and should be valuable guides.

QUOTATIONS

I am using a quotation that contains a second quote within it. How do I handle the citation?
Let's say your paper includes the following sentence:

> According to David M. Kennedy, Roosevelt began his new presidency "by reassuring his countrymen that 'this great nation will endure as it has endured, will revive and will prosper.... The only thing we have to fear ... is fear itself.' "

Of course, you'll cite Kennedy, but do you need to cite *his* source for the Roosevelt quote? No. It's not required. In some cases, however, your readers will benefit from a little extra information about the quote within a quote. You can easily do that in your footnote or endnote:

> [99] Kennedy, *Freedom from Fear*, 134. The Roosevelt quote comes from his 1933 inaugural address.

I am quoting from some Spanish and French books and doing the translations myself. How should I handle the citations?
Just include the words "my translation" immediately after the quote or in the citation. You don't need to do this each time. After the first quotation, you can tell your readers that you are translating all quotes yourself. Then cite the foreign-language text you are using.

---

1. Ralph Berry, *The Research Project: How to Write It* (London: Routledge, 2000), 108–9.

In some papers, you might want to include quotes in both the original and translation. That's fine. Either the translation or the original can come first; the other follows in parentheses or brackets. For instance:

> In Madame Pompadour's famous phrase, "Après nous, le déluge." (After us, the flood.) As it turned out, she was right.

ELECTRONIC MATERIALS AND MICROFILM

Some citations list "microfilm." Others list "microform" or "microfiche." What's the difference? Do I need to mention any of them in my citations? They are all tiny photographic images, read with magnifying tools. Libraries use these formats to save money and storage space for large document collections. *All* these images are called *microforms*, no matter what material they are stored on. When they are stored on reels of film, they're called *microfilm*. When they are stored on plastic sheets or cards, they're called *microfiche*.

When you use materials that have been photographically reduced like this, you should say so in the citation, just as you do for Web sites or electronic information. (If the microforms simply reproduce printed material exactly, some citation styles allow you to cite the printed material directly. But you are always safe if you mention that you read it on microfilm or microfiche. The same is true for citing print items that are reproduced electronically.)

The URL I'm citing is long and needs to go on two lines. How do I handle the line break?
Here's the technical answer. If the URL takes up more than one line, break *after* a

- slash
- double slash

break *before* a

- period
- comma
- question mark
- tilde (~)
- ampersand (&)
- hyphen

- underline
- number sign

Here are some examples:

Full URL	http://www.charleslipson.com/index.htm
Break after slash	http://www.charleslipson.com/
	index.htm
Break before	http://www.charleslipson
other	.com/index.htm
punctuation	

These "break rules" apply to all citation styles.

There's a rationale for these rules. If periods, commas, or hyphens come at the end of a line, they might be mistaken for punctuation marks. By contrast, when they come at the beginning of a line, they are clearly part of the URL. To avoid confusion, don't add hyphens to break long words in the URL.

You can produce such breaks in two ways. One is to insert a line break by pressing the shift-enter keys simultaneously, at least on Windows-based systems. Alternatively, you can insert a space in the URL so your word-processing program automatically wraps the URL onto two lines. (Without such a space, the word processor would force the entire URL onto one line.)

Even though you are technically allowed to break URLs before periods, commas, and hyphens, I try to avoid such breaks because these punctuation marks are easy to overlook and confuse readers. Instead, I try to break only after a slash or double slash, and then only when I am printing the final version of the paper. When I'm sending it electronically, I try to avoid breaks altogether. That way, the recipient will have "live" hyperlinks to click on.

Tips on citing Web pages: As you take notes, write down the

- URL for the Web site or Web page
- Name or description of the page or site
- Date you accessed it

Writing the name or description of a Web site is useful because if the URL changes (as they sometimes do), you still can find it by searching.

As for the access date, some citation styles, such as APA and MLA, require it. Others, such as *The Chicago Manual of Style*, make it optional. They tell you to include it only when it's relevant, such as for time-sensitive data.

If sites are particularly useful, add them to your "favorites" list. If you add several sites for a paper, create a new category (or folder) named for the paper and drop the URLs into that. A folder will gather the sites in a single location and keep them from getting lost in your long list of favorites.

SCIENCE CITATIONS

In the sciences, some citations include terms like DOI, PII, and PMID. What are they? Do I need to include them in my citations?
They identify articles within large electronic databases. Just like other parts of your citations, they help readers locate articles and data you have used. In fact, you may use them yourself to return to an article for more research.

Not every scientific journal includes them in citations or lists them for its own articles. Some do; some don't. My advice: When you do research, write the numbers down and consider including them in your own citations. They appear at the very end of each citation, right after the pagination and URL.

What do the various letters mean? DOI stands for digital object identifier. It's an international system for identifying and exchanging digital intellectual property. Like a URL, it can be used to locate an item. Unlike a URL, it remains the same, even if the item is moved to a new location.

PII stands for publisher item identifier. It, too, identifies the article and can be used for search and retrieval.

PMID appears in many medical and biological journals. It stands for PubMed identification. The PubMed database includes virtually all biomedical journals plus some preprints. It is available online at www.ncbi.nlm.nih.gov/entrez and has a tutorial for new users. This invaluable database was developed by the National Center for Biotechnology Information at the National Library of Medicine.

Other specialized fields have their own electronic identifiers. MR, for example, refers to articles in the Mathematical Reviews database. Physics has identifying numbers for preprints (prepublication articles), which classifies them by subfield.

You are not required to list any of these electronic identifiers in your citations, but doing so may help you and your readers.

In the sciences, I'm supposed to abbreviate journal titles. Where do I find these abbreviations?

The easiest way is to look at the first page of the article you are citing. It usually includes the abbreviation and often the full citation for the article. You can also go to various Web sites assembled by reference librarians, listing journal abbreviations in many fields. One useful site is "All That JAS: Journal Abbreviation Sources," compiled and maintained by Gerry McKiernan, Science and Technology Librarian and Bibliographer at Iowa State, http://www.public.iastate.edu/~CYBERSTACKS/JAS.htm.

INDEX